Mendacity in Early Modern Literature and Culture

Mendacity in Early Modern Literature and Culture examines the historical, cultural, and epistemological underpinnings of lying and deception in early modern England, including the political, religious, aesthetic, and philosophical discourses that governed the codes of lying and truth-telling from the sixteenth to the early eighteenth centuries. The contributions to this collection draw on a wide range of early modern English literature from Shakespeare to Swift, and from travel writing to poetry, in order to explore the extent to which plays, poems, and narrative texts in this period were sites of negotiation, and, at times, of ideological warfare between the moral imperative of truth-telling and the expediency of telling lies. What were the cultural norms of truthfulness and lying, and on what basis were they constructed? What were the consequences when someone did not share the assumed common project of truth-telling? And which forms of communication were exempt from the pragmatic strictures on mendacious discourse?

This book was originally published as a special issue of the *European Journal of English Studies*.

Ingo Berensmeyer is Professor of English and American Literature at Justus Liebig University, Giessen, Germany, and Visiting Professor of English Literature and Culture at Ghent University, Belgium. His research interests range from Shakespeare to contemporary literature. His most recent publications are *'Angles of Contingency': Literarische Kultur im England des siebzehnten Jahrhunderts* (2007); study guides to Shakespeare's *Hamlet* (2007) and to *Literary Theory* (2009), and the co-edited book *Perspectives on Mobility* (with Christoph Ehland, 2013).

Andrew Hadfield is Professor of English at the University of Sussex, Brighton, UK, and Visiting Professor at the University of Granada, Spain. He is the author of a number of works on early modern literature, including *Edmund Spenser: A Life* (2012), *Shakespeare and Republicanism* (2005), and *Literature, Travel and Colonialism in the English Renaissance, 1540–1625* (1998). He is vice-chair of the Society for Renaissance Studies and is currently writing a book on lying in early modern England.

Mendacity in Early Modern Literature and Culture

Edited by

Ingo Berensmeyer and Andrew Hadfield

Routledge
Taylor & Francis Group

LONDON AND NEW YORK

First published 2016
by Routledge
2 Park Square, Milton Park, Abingdon, Oxon, OX14 4RN, UK

and by Routledge
711 Third Avenue, New York, NY 10017, USA

Routledge is an imprint of the Taylor & Francis Group, an informa business

British Library Cataloguing in Publication Data
A catalogue record for this book is available from the British Library

ISBN 13: 978-1-138-65178-4

Typeset in Perpetua
by RefineCatch Limited, Bungay, Suffolk

Publisher's Note
The publisher accepts responsibility for any inconsistencies that may have
arisen during the conversion of this book from journal articles to book chapters,
namely the possible inclusion of journal terminology.

Disclaimer
Every effort has been made to contact copyright holders for their permission to
reprint material in this book. The publishers would be grateful to hear from any
copyright holder who is not here acknowledged and will undertake to rectify
any errors or omissions in future editions of this book.

Contents

Citation Information

The chapters in this book were originally published in the *European Journal of English Studies*, volume 19, issue 2 (August 2015). When citing this material, please use the original page numbering for each article, as follows:

Introduction

Mendacity in Early Modern Literature and Culture: An Introduction
Ingo Berensmeyer and Andrew Hadfield
European Journal of English Studies, volume 19, issue 2 (August 2015) pp. 131–147

Chapter 1

Hiding the Peacock's Legs: Rhetoric, Cosmetics and Deception in Shakespeare's Lucrece *and Trussell's* Hellen
Anna Swärdh
European Journal of English Studies, volume 19, issue 2 (August 2015) pp. 148–162

Chapter 2

Mendacity and Kingship in Shakespeare's Henry V *and* Richard III
Eric Pudney
European Journal of English Studies, volume 19, issue 2 (August 2015) pp. 163–175

Chapter 3

'An Anxious Entangling and Perplexing of Consciences': John Donne and Catholic Recusant Mendacity
Shanyn Altman
European Journal of English Studies, volume 19, issue 2 (August 2015) pp. 176–188

Chapter 4

Truth and Lying in Early Modern Travel Narratives: Coryat's Crudities, *Lithgow's* Totall Discourse *and Generic Change*
Kirsten Sandrock
European Journal of English Studies, volume 19, issue 2 (August 2015) pp. 189–203

Chapter 5

'Betrayed My Credulous Innocence': Mendacity and Female Education in John Milton and the 'Battle of the Sexes'
Anne-Julia Zwierlein
European Journal of English Studies, volume 19, issue 2 (August 2015) pp. 204–219

Chapter 6

Lying, Language and Intention: Reflections on Swift
Brean Hammond and Gregory Currie
European Journal of English Studies, volume 19, issue 2 (August 2015) pp. 220–233

For any permission-related enquiries please visit:
http://www.tandfonline.com/page/help/permissions

Note from the Publisher

We would like to note that in Chapter 3, 'An Anxious Entangling and Perplexing of Consciences': John Donne and Catholic Recusant Mendacity, by Shanyn Altman, the following error appears: "'The great relevance of John Donne's *Pseudo-Martyr*,' writes Anthony Raspa (1993, xvii)". The author would like to note that the text should read: "'The great relevance of *Pseudo-Martyr*', writes Anthony Raspa (1993, xvii)".

Shanyn Altman, the author of Chapter 3, 'An Anxious Entangling and Perplexing of Consciences': John Donne and Catholic Recusant Mendacity, also wishes to point the reader towards further work on the subject of living martyrdom in *Pseudo-Martyr*, and in particular the work of Susannah Monta in her book *Martyrdom and Literature in Early Modern England* (Cambridge: CUP, 2005), pp. 131–150.

Ingo Berensmeyer and Andrew Hadfield

MENDACITY IN EARLY MODERN LITERATURE AND CULTURE: AN INTRODUCTION

Lying, cheating and deceiving can safely be assumed to be among the oldest forms of human behaviour. Yet while mendacity is a perennial social practice, its ethical implications have been viewed differently at different times and in varying cultural, political, religious and philosophical contexts. This issue sets out to explore the historical, cultural and epistemological underpinnings of mendacity in early modern England, including political and religious discourses that governed the codes of lying and truth-telling from the sixteenth to the early eighteenth centuries. The essays in this issue allow us to see the extent to which plays, poems and narrative texts in the early modern period were sites of negotiation and, at times, of ideological warfare between the moral imperative of truth-telling and the expediency of telling lies. They draw on English literature from Shakespeare to Swift for their case studies, but their concerns are deliberately not confined to literature in isolation.

With regard to the topic of literature and lying, the early modern period is of particular interest because it is often regarded as a formative period for the emergence of imaginative writing in a modern sense. There is a strong line of thought in literary theory and literary history, following on from the classical tradition, which regards the early modern period as establishing for imaginative writing a relative autonomy from the norms of truth-telling that govern everyday communication: in Sir Philip Sidney's famous phrase, 'of all writers under the sun the poet is the least liar, and, though he would, as a poet can scarcely be a liar' because 'he nothing affirms, and therefore never lieth' (1973: 102).[1] Yet this subtle distinction between factual and fictional discourse, though theoretically present, was difficult to establish and maintain in practice. As the essays gathered here demonstrate, current scholarship is more likely to emphasise the precariousness of this distinction. According to some, the distinction itself has not yet fully emerged at this time; travel writing is one particular genre in which the boundaries between factual and fictional discourse are notably fluid in the early modern period (see the article by Kirsten Sandrock in this issue). According to others, the distinction is there but it is unstable and tends to break down under pressure and in moments of moral, political and religious crisis. Across different genres and forms, early modern writing is entangled in questions of truth and lying that are not easily transcended and that tend, more often than not, towards the paradoxical as a way of describing cognitive dissonance and as a way of decongesting blockage effects.[2] For example, when Shakespeare has Touchstone in *As You Like It* compress the Renaissance debate about truth, falsehood and poetry into the aphorism 'the truest poetry is the most feigning' (3.3.15–16; Shakespeare 1997: 1633), he delivers more than a 'witty deconstruction' of a kind of poetry that is 'designed to deceive, with a view to seduction' (Corcoran, 2010: 153). His pun connects the creation of fictions with erotic desire ('faining'), and in doing so it demonstrates the 'scepticism' which this play, but also many other Renaissance texts, 'extend[s] to questions of truth in language' (Bath, 1986: 31).

The most famous Enlightenment proponent of truth-telling as a moral imperative is certainly Immanuel Kant. Kant's essay '*Über ein vermeintes Recht aus Menschenliebe zu lügen*' (On a Supposed Right to Lie from Altruistic Motives) contains his famous dictum about lying: that even if you are faced with a murderer at your door, your duty is to tell the truth no matter what (Kant, 1949 [1797]: 347). This is a convenient starting point for modern philosophical discussions of mendacity. For Kant, truth-telling is a moral imperative that must on no condition be violated. To lie is to diminish one's status as a human being. According to this view, philosophical enquiry fails fundamentally if it is not underpinned with the basic assumption that each philosopher is telling the truth and is therefore limited simply by his or her errors, which can be pointed out by well-meaning disputants. To lie, to distort and warp an argument for motives other than establishing what is true is to destroy the purpose of human enquiry.

Although lying is not explicitly mentioned in Kant's famous 1784 essay 'An Answer to the Question: "What is Enlightenment?"', the critique of lying is a cornerstone of Kant's understanding of this term. His target in this essay is childishness:

> Enlightenment is man's emergence from his self-incurred immaturity. Immaturity is the inability to use one's own understanding without the guidance of another. This immaturity is self-incurred if its cause is not lack of understanding, but lack of resolution and courage to use it without the guidance of another. The motto of enlightenment is therefore: Sapere aude! Have courage to use your own understanding!
>
> (Kant, 1991: 54)

Kant demands that mankind sweep away anything that interferes with rational, dispassionate enquiry and so become adult. Lack of understanding is one thing, but it is something that can be challenged and eventually solved by confronting the truth when it is pointed out by your peers and teachers; lack of an attempt to try and understand is another. The essay on lying can be read as a companion piece to Kant's 'Enlightenment' essay; it forms a part of the Enlightenment project. Lying, for Kant, needs to be demolished, like the child's condition of immaturity, before proper enlightened enquiry can begin. Lying, in this view, betrays a lack of responsibility to the self and to others. It is an immature reaction to a difficult situation, whether that concerns a minor domestic transgression, a desire not to lose face in front of one's peers in a philosophical argument, or, at the very limits of self-interest, deceiving the murderer at the door. We should not be surprised that other major Enlightenment figures represented themselves in Kantian terms, awakening from a childish need to lie into adult maturity. Perhaps the pivotal moment in Jean-Jacques Rousseau's *Confessions* (1782) – certainly the one that readers remember – occurs when he confesses to lying about the servant girl Marianne. Rousseau had stolen a ribbon, but blamed Marianne, a fellow employee, resulting in her being dismissed without a reference. Her dignified parting words are 'Rousseau, I thought you were a good person. You make me very unhappy, but I would not want to be in your place' (cited in Williams, 2002: 176; original in Rousseau, 2013: 417). The story of the *Confessions* is that of a development from childish self-interest to an adult understanding of the need for enlightenment, which, for Rousseau, meant rediscovering the good that had been buried under layers of self-deception, hence the need for a confession of lies and other sins to purge the past and emerge anew. It is a Kantian project. And is it any accident that the most famous story about the first president of the new country that emerged from the Enlightenment involves the refusal of a child (George Washington) to lie about an event as relatively unimportant as chopping down a cherry tree? This is the sign of a man-boy, one destined to lead not just a country but the new country that redefined the aims of the revolutions that swept through the world in the eighteenth century, as Hannah Arendt has argued (2006).

In the pre-Kantian world of early modern England, however, lying is not usually discussed in terms of a progress from mendacity to honesty or from childhood to adulthood. The best-known discussions about lying in the English Renaissance are not about truth-telling but about equivocation, about how to evade the hostile enquiries of curious authorities without actually lying and thus committing a sin. Thus a treatise like Father Henry Garnett's *Treatise of Equivocation* was designed to perform the neat trick of preventing very bad things, such as torture and execution, without imperilling the equivocator's soul. In this way the treatise as a how-to manual was in line with the views of the most stringent thinkers on lying available in this period, most significantly Saint Augustine. In his *De mendacio*, Augustine argued in ways that bear many similarities to Kant. He is quite clear that lies are an abuse of the ability to speak that God has given us, so they can never be justified. However, in his taxonomy of lying Augustine allows for one exception: lies can be told when they prevent harm to a person (Augustine, 1887). In his example about the murderer Kant is answering Augustine and closing down his one exception.

Garnett's writing can be placed in the same tradition. He clearly does not believe lying to be a good thing, but he tries to show how it can be avoided in extreme situations. He acknowledges that in swearing an oath one must tell the truth, but turns the need to avoid falsehood around for his own purposes:

> Thou shalt swear (sayeth the Prophett Hieremy) our Lord liveth, in trewth and in iudgement, and in justice. Uppon wch place the holy doctor St. Hierom noteth that there must be three companions of euery oath, truth, iudgement, and justice. Of whome all the deuines have learned the same, requiring these three conditions in every lawfull oath, and condemning all oathes wch are made without all or any one of them. The reason heareof is, for that an oath beyng

an invocation of the soueraigne ma^tie of God for testimony of that wch is sworne, wee ought always in such invocations to vse judgement or discretion to see that wee do nothinge rashly, or w^thout dew reverence, devotion, and faith, towards so great a ma^tie. But we must especially regard that wee make not hym, who is the chiefe and soveraigne veritye and inflexible justice, a witnesse of that wch eyther is false or an uniust promise; for otherwise an oath wanting judgement or discretion, and wisedome, is a rashe oath; that wch wanteth justice is called an vniust oath; and that finally, where there is not truthe is *adiudged a false or lyinge oathe, and is more properly then all the rest called Periurye.*

(Garnett, 1851: 6–7, our emphasis)

This is a fascinating and clever piece of casuistry, which comes close to performing what it describes. Trying to avoid the need to lie will result in far worse abuses of truth than actually being duplicitous. Garnett declares his belief in the value of oaths. It is the very truthfulness of the properly sworn oath which leads to an argument in defence of lying. The stronger the need for the truth, the clearer its definition, the more excusable will the lie be. For Garnett, the need for truth only leads to the chance to lie. For Kant the answer would surely have been different: you would explain to the authorities that you were a Jesuit and that you could not possibly swear such an oath and would then take whatever consequences resulted.

Equivocation was the doctrine designed to prevent this undesirable outcome. The aim was for the speaker to be able to preserve their status as a truth-teller before God, while deliberately misleading the authorities, keeping the torturers of this world from your door. In the end God would know that you had tried to do the right thing, as long as you took some precautions to avoid the sort of barefaced lies that troubled Augustine. Garnett clearly enjoys sailing close to the wind, as this cunning and punning example demonstrates:

We may use some equivocall word wch hath many significations, and we vnder-stand it in one sense, wch is trewe, although the hearer conceave the other, wch is false. So did Abraham and Isaac say, that theire wives were theire sisters, wch was not trewe as the hearers vnderstood it, or in the pper meaning, wherby a sister signifyeth one borne of the same father or mother, or of both, but in a general signification, wherby a brother or sister signifyeth one neere of kynred, as Abraham called Lott his brother, who was but his brother's sonne; and our Lord is sayed to haue had brothers and sisters, wheras pperly he had neyther. The like vnto this were if one should be asked whether such a straunger lodgeth in my howse, and I should aunswere, 'he lyeth not in my howse,' meaning that he doth not tell a lye there, althoughe he lodge there.

(48–9)

As before, this is an excellent and witty piece of writing, which illuminates and deceives at the same time, making a serious point if you are sharp enough to read the words correctly. The two examples are not, of course, the same. The first example is a piece of shorthand, whereby a relationship is used to characterise a series of different ones for ease, a synecdoche. Exactly the same process whereby children call favourite friends of their parents 'auntie' or 'uncle' or 'cousin' is used ubiquitously in this period. Then he gives the real example which may be of use to those harbouring priests, a homonym that joins two entirely different meanings: lying, meaning to not tell the truth, and lying, meaning not to stand or sit up, signifying in turn, as a synecdoche, staying. Garnett cannot have written this passage innocently as if the disparity of the examples had not occurred to him. The choice of word 'lying', placed next to three biblical examples, two well-known sibling relationships from the Old Testament, and one involving God himself, suggests a certain brio, a sparkling confidence demonstrated to help inspire an audience who felt themselves under serious threat. This passage suggests that if a Jesuit could write with such insouciance in spite of the constant dangers he faced, then surely all would be well.

A long-time student of religion, Perez Zagorin recognised that the intellectual temper of the Continent was characterised by widespread and wide-ranging modes of such sharp practice. For him, this was the 'Age of Dissimulation' (Zagorin, 1990: 330). He does not make the case but the point is surely that the Age of Dissimulation precedes the Age of Enlightenment. For Zagorin, the story is one of religion and religious identity. Truth-telling/lying constituted a moral and theological problem, with a vast number of Europeans eager to find some way of escaping persecution for heresy, either by adopting a clear-cut belief in a land where religious divisions were straightforward – notably, Spain; adopting a more double-sided belief that could be switched either way as circumstances demanded; or finding a means of saying one thing to the authorities and another to God, as the Jesuits did in England and those labelled the Nicodemites by Jean Calvin did to cope with the deep-seated religious divisions in France. Kant's intervention in the truth/lying problem presupposes a civil society that accepted a public culture beyond that of private religious belief. To imagine the murderer as a feasible interlocutor who had a right to expect the delivery of the truth, one had to accept that public duties existed between subjects that could not be subsumed within disputes about religion. One had to have a public sphere.

Perhaps this is not, strictly speaking, accurate. In Christopher Marlowe's *Tamburlaine, Part Two* (1587–1588), we witness the Christian forces led by Sigismund of Hungary decide to break their oaths to the Turks because making a promise to an infidel is not binding:

> Frederick. Now, then, my lord, advantage take here of,
> And issue suddenly upon the rest:
> That in the fortune of their overthrow,
> We may discourage all the pagan troop,
> That dare attempt to war with Christians.
> Sigismund. But calls not then your grace to memory
> The league we lately made with king Orcanes,
> Confirmed by oaths and articles of peace,
> And calling Christ for record of our truths?
> This should be treachery and violence
> Against the grace of our profession.
> Baldwin. No whit, my lord: for with such infidels,
> In whom no faith nor true religion rests,

We are not bound to those accomplishments,
The holy laws of Christendom enjoin:
But as the faith which they profanely plight
Is not by necessary policy,
To be esteemed assurance for ourselves,
So what we vow to them should not infringe
Our liberty of arms and victory.
Sigismund. Though I confess the oaths they undertake,
Breed little strength to our security,
Yet those infirmities that thus defame
Their faiths, their honours, and religion,
Should not give us presumption to the like.
Our faiths are sound, and must be consummate,
Religious, righteous, and inviolate.
Frederick. Assure your grace, 'tis superstition
To stand so strictly on dispensive faith[.]

(Marlowe, 1971: 2.1.22–49)

Faith overrides any public duty to tell the truth. It is the same case as that made by Garnett in his treatise on equivocation, here represented with rather more drama and dispassion. Marlowe has based his episode on the historical source, but has altered the details so that we can be clear that the breaking of a promise is the issue at stake. The Christian perfidy misfires and they are overwhelmingly defeated by the Turks in battle in the next Act, perhaps a sign that God was really on the side of the Turks, or that he is indifferent to human actions. Marlowe's play came in the wake of Elizabeth's *Act Against Jesuits and Seminarists* (1585), and the execution of Mary Stuart (1587). *Tamburlaine* could therefore be read as an anti-Catholic play, reflecting on the devious practices of those who would undermine the realm with their lies, especially as Marlowe is following John Foxe and Martin Luther's telling, which represents the events in this way (Thomas and Tydeman, 1994: 78). But it does not seem like a play directed at an enemy within or one that champions Christendom against its external enemies: the Turks are able to reflect on the defeat of the Christians and express their shock at their duplicity. The words of Orcanes, King of Natolia, draw attention to the duplicity of the Christians:

Can there be such deceit in Christians,
Or treason in the fleshly heart of man,
Whose shape is figure of the highest God?
Then if there be a Christ, as Christians say,
But in their deeds deny him for their Christ,
If he be son to everliving Jove,
And hath the power of his outstretched arm,
If he be jealous of his name and honour
As is our holy prophet Mahomet,
Take here these papers as our sacrifice
And witness of thy servant's perjury.

(2.1.36–46)

Rather, *Tamburlaine* reads like a critique of bad faith, of self-interest disguised as a holy principle that needs to be exposed and ridiculed.

Was Marlowe, then, ahead of his time? Is *Tamburlaine* advocating the need for public honesty along the lines that Kant was to indicate as necessary? This is hard to tell and it is not as if Marlowe was the only writer who got hot under the collar about dishonesty and double standards. But it is further evidence of the ubiquity of lying as a major issue that defines the Age of Dissimulation, an episode that forces the audience to consider when lying might be appropriate and/or justified. Did Catholics behave any worse than infidels? Did Protestants? Did either of them behave any better? Should any of them be expected to behave any better?

It is possible that we are looking at the problem from the wrong angle or with too narrow a focus. Lying was not simply a problem relating to religion and it may be that Kant's issues with truthfulness in defining his age have another particular source, namely, the practice of rhetoric. The study of rhetoric, as virtually every historian of education, whatever their exact views, has argued, was the focus of the educational reforms of the sixteenth century and characterised educational systems in Europe until the eighteenth century. Concentrating on rhetoric was part of a transformation in school and university teaching that witnessed traditional medieval practices which prepared the educated for clerical life mutate into teaching methods that prepared students for a wider range of professions and careers, teaching them how to write and argue and so be employable as secretaries, bureaucrats, teachers and also writers. As numerous studies – most recently Lynn Enterline's (2012) excellent book on her understanding of Shakespeare's fractious relationship to his experience in the classroom – have pointed out, cultures of education, religion, work and writing were in step. Rhetoric brought with it great benefits: an ability to write, argue and speak in a variety of sophisticated ways for any number of causes, learned through the practice of studying topics in *utramque partem*, on both sides of a question. But it also brought with it attendant anxieties which are, we suspect, in Kant's mind, as characteristics of the culture he wishes to sweep away in favour of a return to logical inquiry. In England, as Peter Mack (2002) has pointed out in his authoritative history of Elizabethan rhetoric, the standard university set text was Quintilian, along with Cicero's speeches, which were the principal examples used in *The Orator's Education*. Quintilian is certainly anxious about the misuse of rhetoric to produce falsehood, but his defence of the art is based on his assertion that the skilful rhetorician will know that he is lying, which proves rather than answers Kant's fears as we understand them. In Book 2, Quintilian responds to objections that rhetoric is not really an art:

> Their second slander is that no art assents to false propositions, because it cannot exist without a cognitive presentation which is invariably true, whereas rhetoric does assent to falsehoods, and therefore is not an art. I am prepared to admit that rhetoric does sometimes say untrue things as if true, but I would not concede that it is therefore in a state of false opinion; there is a great difference between holding an opinion oneself and making someone else adopt it. Generals often use falsehoods: Hannibal, when hemmed in by Fabius, gave the enemy the illusion that his army was in retreat by tying brushwood to the horns of oxen, setting fire to them, and driving the herd at night up

the mountains ... Similarly an orator, when he substitutes a falsehood for the truth, knows it is false and that he is substituting a falsehood for the truth; he does not therefore have a false opinion himself, but he deceives the other person. When Cicero boasted that he had cast a cloud of darkness over the eyes of the jury, in the case of Cluentius, he saw clearly enough himself.

(Quintilian, 2001: I, 385–7)

The passage is characteristic of Quintilian's style and method: a definition followed by an illustrative example. But here, one suspects, the educator is less than comfortable with what he is forced to admit. Rhetoric does not deceive those educated in rhetoric who know how to use and read it correctly. But it can and does mislead others who are taken in by its wiles. Rhetoric can be an art of lying. The example of Hannibal's skilful generalship does not really help as this is an extreme case in which the deceiver is placed in a position in which deception is the best pragmatic course. It does not answer the question of how a rhetorician may deceive an audience when he simply wants to or whether rhetoric can be used to defend tyranny rather than republicanism or democracy. The second example of Cicero bamboozling a jury and openly boasting of his triumph brings us back to the Platonic problem of the philosophical pursuit of truth pitted against the wiles of rhetoric, an issue that this passage acknowledges but does little to solve.

In the concluding book of *The Orator's Education*, Quintilian tries to resolve this dilemma through his contention that Cato's definition of the orator as 'a good man, skilled in speaking' should define the process of creating the *homo rhetoricus*. But the door is open to the old charge that the art of rhetoric is the art of lying. And, indeed, this was precisely the anxiety that would not go away. Only one substantial treatise on lying was printed in sixteenth-century England, *a Politique discourses upon trueth and lying An instruction to princes to keepe their faith and promise: containing the summe of Christian and morall philosophie, and the duetie of a good man in sundrie politique discourses vpon the trueth and lying*. This translation of an original work by Martyn Coignet, published in 1586, was produced by Sir Edward Hoby, the nephew of the translator of Castiglione. We would suggest that, although separated by over 20 years, the two works should be seen as related projects, part of a series of shared interests in behaviour, conduct and the relationship between the self and truth/lies. While Sir Thomas Hoby's translation deals with public performance and disguise, Sir Edward's adopts what we might think of as a maximalist definition of lying, one that provides a simple – and unworkable – answer to the dilemma outlined by Quintilian.

Coignet follows an Augustinian definition of truth as an imitation of God:

for so much as there is nothing more proper to man, being formed according to the image of God, than in his words and manners to approche him the nearest that he is able, & to make his words serue for no other ende, than to declare his good intent & meaning, whereby he may be better able to informe his neighbour.

(Coignet, 1586: 1)

Lying, as Coignet recognises, is the opposite of truth. Again, he follows Augustine, but a precise definition proves elusive:

> So haue we of purpose discoursed of the trueth, before we com to shew the vice of lying, the which we may define by a contrary signification vnto the truth when one speaketh of things vncertain, contrarie to that which one knoweth, making them seeme other then they are. S. Augustin writeth to Consentius, that it is a false significatiom of spech, with a wil to deceiue.
>
> (127)

Coignet accepts that even speaking the truth is a hazardous enterprise and open to misinterpretation, which was what persuaded poor, silly Lucrece to commit suicide, so fearful was she of the malign readings of her fate by the mob. Coignet is, yet again, following Augustine, who famously condemned Lucrece for the un-Christian manner of her death. Coignet reproduces Plato's strictures against poets and painters:

> Painting is a dumme Poesie, and a Poesie is a speaking painting: & the actions which the Painters set out with visible colours and figures, the Poets recken with wordes as though they had in deede beene perfourmed. And the ende of eche is, but to yeeld pleasure by lying, not esteeming the sequele and custome, or impression, which hereby giue to the violating of the lawes and corruption of good manners.
>
> (160)

Coignet finds it easy to divide the world into the truthful good and the wickedness of lying. Accordingly, theatres are also wrong, as are flatterers and the passions. In order to make his case, Coignet has to cast Cicero, whose work is cited sparingly, in a particular role at odds with his significance in Quintilian:

> Cicero was of opinion that there was no difference betweene the lyar and the periured person, and that God had ordained to eche like punishment, and that he which was accustomed to lye, did easily periure himselfe. The which opinion sundry doctors of the church haue in like sort helde.
>
> (131)

A number of questions might be asked about this. Does Coignet know what he is doing in flattening out the material he is citing? Whereas the exponent of rhetoric, Quintilian, is honest about the problem at the heart of his enterprise, Coignet could well be accused of being dishonest about his, perhaps even of lying in his attempt to make everything black and white. What Coignet does might simply be the effect of the common practice of citing a series of authorities. The danger is that the ancients – here as elsewhere – can be looted for juicy quotations, and so all sound the same, saying exactly what the author wants them to say. This is clearly the case here, so that Cicero is cited in Quintilian as the great exponent of rhetoric who admits that eloquence can lead one into deception, deception which can only be the result of lying. Coignet is more eager to maintain his case and to preserve a clear distinction between truth and lies, so he cites Cicero as a harsh opponent of any attempt to soften these divisions. The problem is that in order to do so he undoubtedly misuses his authorities and so either misleads the reader because he does not understand the truth of what he is saying or he deliberately misleads them and so lies. Coignet may not mean to be a rhetorician like Cicero or Castiglione but that is what he is.

Moreover, in rejecting literature *tout court*, Coignet is rejecting one of the most obvious places where discussions of lying could take place. Literary texts, not being bound by the need to be truthful and so not forced to lead the reader to a definite conclusion, could explore the meaning, significance and effects of lying in much more nuanced ways than those bound by rules of truth and lying. Indeed, precisely because they were already involved in discussions of truth and lying regarding their very existence, literary texts invariably foreground these very debates. An obvious example is *The Faerie Queene*. There are clearly moments of particular significance, although, oddly enough, there is no one single article on Spenser and lying. It is noticeable how infrequently Spenser actually uses the words 'lie', 'lying' or 'liar', although it is clear that he is writing about identical, similar or related phenomena. Take three examples:

> For that old man of pleasing wordes had store,
> And well could file his tongue as smooth as glas;
> He told of Saintes and Popes, and euermore
> He strowd an Aue-Mary after and before.

> (Spenser, 2001: I.i.35, 6–9)

Is Archimago actually lying here? An interesting point. He is clearly deceiving them in the narrator's eyes (can we trust the narrator?) and the image that he could file his tongue as smooth as glass is clearly the opposite of truth-telling and so lying if we believe Coignet, not necessarily if we follow Quintilian. Then again, does it matter if he is lying anyway? Isn't what he is doing just as bad even if it cannot be defined as lying, as, if we accept the truth of Protestantism this is all Romish lies, as Protestant polemicists such as John Bale state frequently enough? Or is Spenser deliberately avoiding using the term because what he is saying is not quite what you think?

> An equally well-known example is the following:
> There as they entred at the Scriene, they saw
> Some one, whose tongue was for his trespasse vyle
> Nayld to a post, adiudged so by law:
> For that therewith he falsely did reuyle,
> And foule blaspheme that Queene for forged guyle,
> Both with bold speaches, which he blazed had,
> And with lewd poems, which he did compyle;
> For the bold title of a Poet bad
> He on himselfe had ta'en, and rayling rymes had sprad.

Thus there he stood, whylest high ouer his head,
There written was the purport of his sin,
In cyphers strange, that few could rightly read,
BON FONT: but bon that once had written bin,
Was raced out, and Mal was now put in.
So now Malfont was plainely to be red;
Eyther for th'euill, which he did therein,
Or that he likened was to a welhed
Of euill words, and wicked sclaunders by him shed.

(V.ix.25–6)

Note that here, Spenser uses a whole series of words defining and explicating deception and deceitfulness: 'blaspheme', 'forged guyle', 'bold', 'blazed', 'lewd', 'rayling', cyphers', 'euill words' and 'wicked sclaunders', but he never once actually says the poet lies. We are told that we can read this incident clearly now that the poet's name is given in black capitals, but we are not actually told that he does not tell the truth, that he lies about anything. What he says may offend people and seem misleading as well as offensive. But it may well be true.

The caveat is clearly important. What we witness in *The Faerie Queene* is a language about deception, about truth and lying, that very rarely mentions the word 'lie', even when you imagine that it might do. Indeed, apart from one quibble on 'lying', meaning remaining supine and failing to tell the truth, as appeared later in Garnett's equivocation treatise, the word 'lie' only appears twice in the long poem (although then pun remains active throughout). Scudamore accuses Duessa of lying when she reappears at the start of Book IV but the most significant example surely occurs very near the end of Book VI, when Calidore approaches the Blatant Beast:

Tho when the Beast saw, he mote nought auaile,
By force, he gan his hundred tongues apply,
And sharpely at him to reuile and raile,
With bitter termes of shamefull infamy;
Oft interlacing many a forged lie,
Whose like he neuer once did speake, nor heare,
Nor euer thought thing so vnworthily[.]

(VI.xii.33, 1–7)

At last, we have the truth about lying, because we have known all along that Book VI is really about this issue which is inextricably related to courtesy and courteous behaviour (again, you can see why it is no surprise that the Hobys want to think about truth and lies alongside courtly behaviour). Courtesy is the root of 'civil conversation' but the Knight of Courtesy loves 'simple truth and stedfast honesty', two definitions that are not necessarily at odds but which might be and which also raise the spectre of the binary divisions established by Coignet following Augustine. Rhetoric is the basis of the art of civil conversation so it is important to note that Spenser locates the problem of truth/falsehood here rather than in debates about religion. For Coignet, lying is an offence against God and one's neighbours, but Spenser seems to turn these common assumptions upside down. It is only when the beast attacks and despoils a monastery that s/he is defined as a liar. As with *Tamburlaine*, it is not clear that the text supports an easy and satisfying discourse of religious truth and diabolic lies even when it seems to. Ben Jonson suggested that Spenser was attacking the Puritans when he represented the Beast rampaging through the established church (Cummings, 1971: 136), but the truth may be more complicated, with Spenser showing how practices of lying lead eventually to sacrilege, not vice versa.

What we witness in Book VI of *The Faerie Queene* is the initially comic and eventually terrifying realisation that there is no central concept of truth, nothing that holds everything together as Coignet asserts that there is (God, the monarch). Calidore is forced to 'tread an endlesse trace withouten guyde' because he is supposed to be courteous and follow the truth without any means of connecting the two in a coherent model established by a strong central authority. Calidore is clueless and situations drift so that we are not sure what the truth actually is. He comes across Calepine and Serena *in flagrante delicto*, which leads to a comic series of misunderstandings:

> With which his gentle words and goodly wit
> He soone allayd that Knights conceiu'd displeasure,
> That he besought him downe by him to sit,
> That they mote treat of things abrode at leasure;
> And of aduentures, which had in his measure
> Of so long waies to him befallen late.
> So downe he sate, and with delightfull pleasure
> His long aduentures gan to him relate,
> Which he endured had through daungerous debate.
>
> Of which whilest they discoursed both together,
> The faire Serena (so his Lady hight)
> Allur'd with myldnesse of the gentle wether,
> And pleasaunce of the place, the which was dight
> With diuers flowres distinct with rare delight,
> Wandred about the fields, as liking led
> Her wauering lust after her wandring sight,
> To make a garland to adorne her hed,
> Without suspect of ill or daungers hidden dred.

(VI.iii.20–1)

Certainly Calidore exercises his skills in 'civil conversation' and appears to get himself out of an embarrassing situation. But surely things cannot be quite as they seem: the opening lines are arch in the extreme, as is the description of Serena wandering off because it's a lovely day. This is a situation of extreme embarrassment and either the people involved are a bit odd or they really don't mind such an interruption (perhaps a straw poll of the audience could establish this once and for all?). It is likely, therefore, either that the narrator is lying to us or that Calepine is lying to Calidore, having to act courteously and hide the truth of his feelings. A mild enough example, of course, but one that shows just how out of joint the times are for equating truth and courtesy against lying and falsehood. And the Blatant Beast, later a figure of lying itself, then appears to whisk Serena away, a sign that we are witnessing the slippery slope from white social lies to ones of cosmic significance.

Spenser was not, needless to say, alone in thinking about lies and lying – almost any number of authors could be summoned to make a similar case. But what is especially interesting about Spenser's writing is that he does not base his understanding of lying and its significance on religion. In fact, after an initial opening book about Holiness, *The Faerie Queene* moves ever further away from religion, suggesting that Zagorin's understanding of the early modern period as an 'Age of Dissimulation' is indeed right, but that religion is probably not all we need to think about. The culture of lying went much further.

Later, towards the end of the seventeenth century, at the time of the 'Glorious Revolution', which implemented a more liberal cultural ideology, including (for Protestants, at least) religious toleration, social and political pressures towards dissimulation moved away from faith altogether and were funnelled into the philosophical and moral terms of common sense and politeness. One need only point to Locke's *Essay concerning Human Understanding* to realise the extent to which the promotion of a plain style paves the way for a Kantian highmindedness about rhetoric, which is understood as an 'Abuse of Words' and nothing but a 'powerful instrument of Error and Deceit':

> But yet, if we would speak of Things as they are, we must allow, that all the Art of Rhetorick, besides Order and Clearness, all the artificial and figurative application of Words Eloquence hath invented, are for nothing else but to insinuate wrong Ideas, move the Passions, and thereby mislead the Judgment; and so indeed are perfect cheat[.]
>
> (3.10.34, Locke, 1979: 508)

John Dryden, in his *Religio Laici* (1682), concurs that '[a] Man is to be cheated into Passion, but to be reason'd into Truth' (1972: 109). The antinomy of passion and reason continues into the eighteenth century, particularly in discourses concerning the epistemological problem of 'enthusiasm', as in Shaftesbury's *Sensus Communis* (1709; cf. Heyd, 1995). Because, for Locke and many of his contemporaries, language is predominantly a social and intersubjective medium of exchange, 'the great Bond that holds Society together' (*Essay* 3.11.11, Locke, 1979: 509), questions of style and propriety also have important social and political implications. In England in particular, after the perceived excesses of religious fundamentalism and puritanism during the Civil War and 'Interregnum', it was a predominant concern to curb any such extremes for the sake of maintaining what Dryden called 'Common quiet' (1972: 122). Ideals of civility and sociability, including plain speaking and truth-telling, are upheld in order to accommodate or, if necessary, suppress political and religious differences in order to banish the spectre of civil war and to hold the Hobbesian state of nature at bay – where, we may assume, lying would have been *du jour* as a common weapon in the war of everyone against everyone else. (According to Hobbes in *De homine* 10.3 [Hobbes, 1839: 91–92], the ability to lie is one distinguishing feature between human beings and other animals.) The Restoration comedy of manners, from Etherege's *Man of Mode* to Congreve's *The Way of the World*, thrives on the double standard of, on the one hand, an official culture of plain dealing and plain speaking, and, on the other hand, of the regular employment of lies and general manipulative behaviour as a means to achieve social goals.

The Enlightenment dream of a perfect society with no need for lying or deceit is part of a utopian tradition that includes Montaigne's essay 'Of the Cannibals', which claims that these inhabitants of the New World had no use for lying: 'The very words that import lying, falshood, treason, dissimulations, covetousness, envie, detraction, and pardon, were never heard amongst them' (1910: 1, 220). The distance between that world and ours is – painfully, though humorously – marked by Swift's *Gulliver's Travels*, in which only the Houyhnhnms are incapable of telling lies. In their essay for this volume, Brean Hammond and Gregory Currie explore what this tells us about Swift's attitude towards truth and mendacity in the context of early eighteenth-century politics and imaginative writing; they also engage in an interdisciplinary debate, highly appropriate for this discussion of early modern mendacity, between literature, linguistics and philosophy. Readers will also find it useful to compare this perspective on Swift's satirical travel-writing with Kirsten Sandrock's exploration of how generic conventions in English Renaissance travel literature change 'from mendacity to veracity'. In her view, early modern travel writing inhabits a transitional boundary zone between fictional and non-fictional modes of reading and writing. Reading two texts from the early seventeenth century, Coryat's *Crudities* and Lithgow's *Totall Discourse*, she shows how the travelogue in this period negotiates uneasy and unstable compromises between an emerging convention of factuality in travel-writing and a residual discourse of myth-making and fiction.

In her article on 'John Donne and Catholic Recusant Mendacity', Shanyn Altman argues that the religious division wrought by the Reformation made the need to lie a fact of life for many early modern English men and women. People may have condemned duplicity and mendacity as abstract vices and pledged a need to articulate the truth, but King James's imposition of the Oath of Allegiance on his subjects meant that many had to mislead in order to survive, as John Donne recognised in his treatise urging Catholics not to seek death for their cause, *Pseudo-Martyr*. Anna Swärdh explores a very different kind of deception in two narrative poems, Shakespeare's *Rape of Lucrece* and John Trussell's rather less celebrated *First Rape of Fair Hellen*, published a year later (1595). Swärdh shows how rhetoric, an art that could lead to truth or deception, enabled virtuous women to disguise their vulnerability and so protect themselves, and also exposed the dishonest strategies of their rapacious pursuers. Equally nuanced is Eric Pudney's exploration of kingship in Shakespeare's *Henry V* and *Richard III*, which also shows how literary works emerge from a humanist culture based on rhetorical training and argument. While *Henry V*'s lies can be read as strategically useful deceptions for a higher purpose, those of *Richard III* cannot be redeemed and almost become ends in themselves. Concentrating on a later text, Anne-Julia Zwierlein explores the troubling question of Milton's representation of Eve in *Paradise Lost* and her role in the Fall of Mankind. Zwierlein finds that Milton's interest in science and scientific language forms a crucial context for our understanding of Eve's transformation to a fallen woman, especially if one reads her against the virtuous lady in *Comus*. Eve's inability to understand Satan's rhetorical sleights of hand allied to her natural curiosity lead to disaster as she cannot understand the truth, a pointed contrast to the insight of the lady who can spot mendacity when she sees it.

Taken together, the essays in this issue challenge supra-historical or ahistorical views of truth-telling as a universal norm. They explore the particular ways in which codes of truth and falsehood are embedded in early modern English culture, and the ways in which they were subject to historical and cultural change. They investigate the cultural norms of truthfulness and lying that were valid during this period, and the basis on which they were constructed. And while this can only be the starting point for a more extended conversation, they also return us to the question of the role, or roles, that imaginative writing was able to play in this construction.

Disclosure statement

No potential conflict of interest was reported by the authors.

Notes

1. This introduction is not the place to discuss the concept of fictionality in the early modern period in detail, nor the competing theories of fiction in modern philosophy and literary theory. For an exemplary discussion of both, based on early modern pastoral poetry, see Iser (1993), and also cf. Pfeiffer (1990) and Berensmeyer (2003). Both Currie (1990) and Walton (1990) offer philosophical perspectives on fiction as a form of 'make-believe'. For the historical origins of fictional discourse in classical antiquity, see Gill and Wiseman (1993). For a related discussion of literature and lying in the early modern period, see Hadfield (2014).
2. This way of putting it is indebted to sociological systems theory; see in particular Teubner (2011), who in turn refers to Gumbrecht and Pfeiffer (1988). For reasons of space, we have to neglect the important distinction between logical and rhetorical paradoxes here. The topic of Renaissance paradox is explored, for example, in Platt (2009).

References

Arendt, Hannah (2006). *On Revolution*. Harmondsworth: Penguin.

Augustine of Hippo (1887). *De Mendacio/on Lying*. Trans. H. Browne. From Nicene and Post-Nicene Fathers, first series, vol. 3. Ed. Philip Schaff. Buffalo, NY: Christian Literature Publishing. Accessed 9 September 2013. <http://www.logicmuseum.com/authors/augustine/demendacio/demendacio.htm>.

Bath, Michael (1986). 'Weeping Stags and Melancholy Lovers: The Iconography of as You like It, II. I.' *Emblematica* 1: 13–52.

Berensmeyer, Ingo (2003). 'No Fixed Address: Pascal, Cervantes, and the Changing Function of Literary Communication in Early Modern Europe.' *New Literary History* 34.4: 623–37.

Coignet, Martyn (1586). *Politique Discourses upon Trueth and Lying an Instruction to Princes to Keepe Their Faith and Promise: Containing the Summe of Christian and Morall Philosophie, and the Duetie of a Good Man in Sundrie Politique Discourses Vpon the Trueth and Lying.*

Corcoran, Neil (2010). *Shakespeare and the Modern Poet.* Cambridge: Cambridge UP.

Cummings, Robert, ed. (1971). *Edmund Spenser: The Critical Heritage.* London: Routledge.

Currie, Gregory (1990). *The Nature of Fiction.* Cambridge: Cambridge UP.

Dryden, John (1972). *Poems, 1681–1684.* Vol. 2. Ed. H.T. Swedenberg Jr. Berkeley/Los Angeles/London: University of California Press.

Enterline, Lynne (2012). *Shakespeare's Schoolroom: Rhetoric, Discipline, Emotion.* Philadelphia, PA: University of Pennsylvania Press.

Garnett, Henry (1851). *A Treatise of Equivocation.* Ed. David Jardine. London: Longman.

Gill, Christopher and Wiseman, T.P., eds (1993). *Lies and Fiction in the Ancient World.* Exeter: U of Exeter P.

Gumbrecht, Hans Ulrich and Pfeiffer, K. Ludwig, eds (1988). *Materialities of Communication.* Trans. William Whobrey. Stanford: Stanford UP.

Hadfield, Andrew (2014). 'Lying in Early Modern Culture.' *Textual Practice* 28.3: 339–63.

Heyd, Michael (1995). *'Be Sober and Reasonable.' The Critique of Enthusiasm in the Seventeenth and Early Eighteenth Centuries.* Leiden: Brill.

Hobbes, Thomas (1839 [1658]). *De homine. Vol. 2 of Thomae Hobbes malmesburiensis opera philosophica quae latine scripsit omnia.* Ed. William Molesworth. London: Bohn.

Iser, Wolfgang (1993). *Renaissance Pastoralism as a Paradigm of Literary Fictionality. The Fictive and the Imaginary. Charting Literary Anthropology.* Baltimore: Johns Hopkins UP. 22–86.

Kant, Immanuel (1949 [1797]). 'On a Supposed Right to Lie from Altruistic Motives.' *Critique of Practical Reason and Ohter Writings in Moral Philosophy.* Ed. and Trans. Lewis White Beck. Chicago, IL: U of Chicago P. 346–50.

Kant, Immanuel (1991). *Political Writings.* Ed. H.S. Reiss. Cambridge: Cambridge UP.

Locke, John (1979). *An Essay concerning Human Understanding.* Ed. Peter H. Nidditch. Oxford: Oxford UP.

Mack, Peter (2002). *Elizabethan Rhetoric: Theory and Practice.* Cambridge: Cambridge University Press.

Marlowe, Christopher (1971). *Tamburlaine.* Ed. J.W. Harper. London: A. C. Black.

Montaigne, Michel de (1910). *The Essayes of Michel Lord of Montaigne.* Trans. John Florio (1603). 3 vols. London: Dent.

Pfeiffer, K. Ludwig (1990). 'Fiction: On the Fate of a Concept between Philosophy and Literary Theory.' *Aesthetic Illusion: Theoretical and Historical Approaches.* Eds Frederick Burwick and Walter Pape. Berlin/New York: de Gruyter. 92–104.

Platt, Peter G. (2009). *Shakespeare and the Culture of Paradox.* Farnham/Burlington, VA: Ashgate.

Quintilian (2001). *The Orator's Education.* Vols. 4. Trans. Donald A. Russell. Cambridge, MA/London: Harvard UP.

Rousseau (2013). *The Essential Writings of Rousseau.* Trans. Peter Constantine. New York: Random House.

Shakespeare, William (1997). *The Norton Shakespeare. Based on the Oxford Edition.* General Ed. Stephen Greenblatt. New York/London: Norton.

Sidney, Philip (1973). 'A Defence of Poetry.' *Miscellaneous Prose of Sir Philip Sidney*. Eds Katherine Duncan-Jones and Jan van Dorsten. Oxford: Clarendon Press. 73–121.

Spenser, Edmund (2001). *The Faerie Queene*. Ed. A.C. Hamilton. Harlow: Longman.

Teubner, Gunther (2011). *Networks as Connected Contracts*. Trans. Michelle Everson. Hart: Oxford.

Thomas, Vivien and Tydeman, William (1994). *Christopher Marlowe: The Plays and Their Sources*. London: Routledge.

Walton, Kendall L. (1990). *Mimesis as Make-believe. On the Foundations of the Representational Arts*. Cambridge, MA/London: Harvard UP.

Williams, Bernard (2002). *Truth and Truthfulness: An Essay in Genealogy*. Princeton UP: Princeton.

Zagorin, Perez (1990). *Ways of Lying. Dissimulation, Persecution, and Conformity in Early Modern Europe*. Cambridge, MA/London: Harvard UP.

Ingo Berensmeyer is Professor of English and American Literature at Justus Liebig University Giessen and Visiting Professor of English Literature and Culture at Ghent University, where he is co-director of the RAP group (Research on Authorship as Performance) and co-editor of the electronic journal *Authorship*. His research interests are in Shakespeare and the early modern period, literary theory and aesthetics, media and cultural ecology, and Britain in the 1950s. His most recent publications are: '*Angles of Contingency': Literarische Kultur im England des siebzehnten Jahrhunderts* (2007); a study guide to Shakespeare's *Hamlet* (2007), *Literary Theory: An Introduction to Approaches, Methods and Terms* (2009) and the co-edited book *Perspectives on Mobility* (with Christoph Ehland, 2013).

Andrew Hadfield is Professor of English at the University of Sussex and Visiting Professor at the University of Granada. He is the author of a number of works on early modern literature, including *Edmund Spenser: A Life* (Oxford, 2012), *Shakespeare and Republicanism* (Cambridge University Press, 2005, paperback, 2008) and *Literature, Travel and Colonialism in the English Renaissance, 1540–1625* (Oxford University Press, 1998, paperback, 2007). He is vice-chair of the Society for Renaissance Studies and is currently writing a book on lying in early modern England.

Anna Swärdh

HIDING THE PEACOCK'S LEGS: RHETORIC, COSMETICS AND DECEPTION IN SHAKESPEARE'S *LUCRECE* AND TRUSSELL'S *HELLEN*

This essay explores rhetorical and cosmetic deception in William Shakespeare's The Rape of Lucrece *(1594) and John Trussell's* Raptus I Helenae. The First Rape of Faire Hellen *(1595). The essay focuses on instances of 'colouring' and 'cloaking' in the poems, terms used by contemporary rhetoricians to describe their art, to show how tensions between rhetorical skill and anxieties related to rhetorical deception are played out. Shakespeare and Trussell both employ narratorial commentary together with cloaking imagery to mark the rapists' rhetorical dissembling as morally despicable, whereas other strategies are used to portray the women's rhetorical and cosmetic cloaking and colouring as more defensible, if not completely unambiguous, forms of self-representation.*

'Let her have shame that cannot closely act', Rosamond is told in Samuel Daniel's vogue-setting poem from 1592, *The Complaint of Rosamond*. The 'seeming Matrone' who helps seduce her into becoming the king's mistress uses various arguments, among them the idea that seeming or acting chaste is always more important than being chaste (Daniel, 1930: 216, 285).[1] The problem of authenticity is central to the complaint poems that followed on Daniel's in the 1590s, all dealing with the delicate task of defending a fallen woman in a setting of rhetorical self-representation. In these poems, we find explicit comments on the duplicitousness of rhetoric but also constant references to seeming versus being, to masking and hiding, and to cosmetics. In this essay I focus on rhetoric as deception in two complaints, William Shakespeare's *The Rape of Lucrece* (1594) and John Trussell's *Raptus I Helenae. The First Rape of Faire Hellen* (1595).[2] What singles these two texts out from the complaint group is their repeated employment of the terms 'cloaking' and 'colouring', terms that are used at the time by rhetoricians to describe their art and denoting concealment as well as rhetorical embellishment.[3] Shakespeare's and Trussell's use of these terms signals the poets' rhetorical self-awareness as well as consciousness of the moral ambiguity inherent in the art of rhetorical persuasion.

Suspicions about rhetoric were regularly expressed in the early modern period, and rhetorical dissimulation was part of a larger context that has been called 'a culture of secrecy' by Jon Snyder (Snyder, 2009), and described in terms of 'dissimulation' by Perez Zagorin (Zagorin, 1990). A central text of early modern rhetorical culture is Baldassare Castiglione's *The Courtier* (1528, translated into English in 1561), with its stress on *sprezzatura*, the 'certain nonchalance which conceals all artistry and makes whatever one says or does seem uncontrived and effortless' (Castiglione, 1967: 67; cf. Snyder, 2009: 70–8). With its focus on the concealment of any art or skill that one possesses, *The Courtier* presents rhetorical skill as part of a larger enterprise of courtly self-representation and deception. In the same vein, as Frank Wigham and Wayne A. Rebhorn point out, George Puttenham in his *Art of English Poesy* (1589) defines all figures of speech as deceptions, 'as deliberate attempts by the writer or speaker to "make our talk more guileful and abusing"' (2007: 55). Andrew Hadfield points to one classical and one early modern source to exemplify the anxieties surrounding rhetoric in the early modern period. Quintilian, author of the extremely influential *Institutio oratoria*, is 'repeatedly anxious about the abuse of rhetoric to produce falsehood', and the same fear that the art of rhetoric is the art of lying 'characterises the anxieties expressed throughout the one substantial treatise on lying that was printed in sixteenth-century England', Mathieu Coignet's *A Politic Discourse upon Truth and Lying* (1586) (Hadfield, 2013: 139).

While Lucrece employs verbal rhetoric in Shakespeare's poem, Trussell's Helen uses make-up to achieve her goals; and the same fears of deception that surrounded rhetoric in the early modern period clung to cosmetics. Castiglione finds make-up acceptable as long as it is used in moderation, even if the clean face is most attractive to men, 'who are always afraid of being deceived by art' (Castiglione, 1967: 86). As Farah Karim-Cooper observes, the problem is the same, that of distinguishing between art and artfulness, in rhetorical as well as cosmetic embellishment (2006: 132–5). The connection between rhetorical and cosmetic ornamentation was frequently made at the time, often, as in Claudius' speech in *Hamlet*, verbalising worries about wrongful deception: 'The harlot's cheek, beautified with plast'ring art, / Is not more ugly to the thing that helps it / Than is my deed to my most painted word' (Shakespeare, 2003: 3.1.52–4). As we shall see, through her use of cosmetics Trussell's Helen can be read as an embodiment of rhetorical embellishment.

With their interest in authenticity and deception, the complaint poems of the 1590s participate in the contemporary culture of rhetorical self-representation and dissimulation, working against as well as within anxieties about the deceptive power of rhetoric belonging to that culture. Starting from the figure of paradiastole (redescribing vices as virtues), this essay will explore instances of 'colouring' and 'cloaking' found in Shakespeare's and Trussell's poems, to show how tensions between rhetorical skill and anxieties related to rhetorical deception are played out in Lucrece's and Helen's stories.

Tarquin and Theseus, Jove and Brutus

As several critics have pointed out, rhetoric and rhetorical training are central to Shakespeare's *Lucrece* (among them Dubrow, 1987; Enterline, 2000; Ellis, 2003;

Roe, 2006; Greenstadt, 2010; Weaver, 2012). The words 'orator' and 'oratory' occur five times in the poem, and we find references to reading, books, tales, schools, eloquence, words, cipher, debate and disputation. When colouring and cloaking occur in the poem, it is often in close vicinity to words related to rhetoric, signalling what was at the time a well-established connection. Similarly, in their manuals and guides, rhetoricians speak of their art in a language borrowed from the fields of painting, cosmetics and clothing. In *The English Secretorie* (1586), Angel Day opens the epistle dedicatory (to Edward de Vere) with two references to skilled painters, deception being a part of Zeuxis' skill:

> ZEUXES endevouring to paint excellentlie, made Grapes in shewe so naturall, that presenting the[m] to view men were deceaved with their shapes and their birds with their cullours. When Apelles drew Venus (though the shew of bewutie seemed woonderful) he daunted not in his workmanship, because he knew his cunning excellent.

Thomas Wilson, in *The Arte of Rhetorique* (1553), writes that elocution 'beautifieth the tongue with great change of colours and variety of figures' (in Vickers, 1999: 120), and in the section on 'Exornation', he advises that 'we may boldly commend and beautify our talk with divers goodly colours and delightful translations, that our speech may seem as bright and precious as a rich stone is fair and orient' (in Vickers, 1999: 123). Puttenham uses both clothing and colouring repeatedly throughout *The Art of English Poesy*: for instance, we are told how 'our vulgar poesy' cannot show itself 'either gallant or gorgeous if any limb be left naked and bare and not clad in his kindly clothes and colours' (Puttenham, 2007: 3.1.221f.).

While rhetorical embellishment was thus generally spoken of in terms of colouring and cloaking, Quentin Skinner has claimed that they are 'the two favourite metaphors' used by rhetoricians to capture specifically the power of the figure of paradiastole to 'disorder the vices and virtues' (Skinner, 2007: 156f.). Richard Sherrey, Angel Day, George Puttenham and Henry Peacham all offer definitions of paradiastole in their rhetorical handbooks, and two of them make use of these metaphors. Peacham defines paradiastole as vices covered in 'the mantles of vertues' (Peacham, 1593: 169; Skinner, 2007: 157), while Day uses the term 'colour' in his definition: '*Paradiastole*, when with a milde interpretation or speech, wee color others or our owne faultes, as when wee call a subtill person, *wise*, a bold fellow, *couragious*, a prodigall man, liberall: a man furious or rash, valiant: a Parasite, a companion: him that is proud, Magnanimous: and such like' (Day, 1592: 90f.). The concepts of colouring and clothing are thus central to the idea of rhetorical embellishment and redescription in early modern England, and they are used with positive as well as negative connotations.

Both Shakespeare's and Trussell's poems include rhetorical redescription of a kind that can be termed paradiastolary, and instances that make use of colouring and cloaking. Such rhetoric is given negative connotations in relation to the rapist men, and can be taken as one strategy the poets use to set up a contrast between unacceptable and acceptable versions of rhetorical dissimulation. In *Lucrece*, the narrator comments on Tarquin's premeditated justification of the rape in terms that define Tarquin's venture as paradiastole:

Thus graceless holds he disputation
'Tween frozen conscience and hot burning will,
And with good thoughts makes dispensation,
Urging the worser sense for vantage still;
Which in a moment doth confound and kill
All pure effects, and doth so far proceed
That what is vile shows like a virtuous deed.

(Shakespeare, 2006: 246–52)

John Roe glosses 'disputes formally' for 'holds ... disputation' (Roe, 2006: note to line 246), placing the section of Tarquin's internal battle, and the particular stanza, squarely within the field of formal rhetorical debate. Tarquin debates with himself for a long time, and at this point the narrator sums up and signals disapproval. Peacham's 1577 description of paradiastole as a figure used 'when vices are excused' (Peacham, 1577: Sig. Niiiiv) is, as Skinner points out, changed to a more negative dismissal in the 1593 edition of *The Garden of Eloquence*, when it is referred to as 'a faulty term of speech' and a 'vice of speech' that is 'a fit instrument of excuse serving to self-love, partial favour, blinde affection, and a shamelesse person, which for the better maintenance of wickednesse useth to cover vices with the mantles of vertues' (Peacham, 1593: 168f.; Skinner, 2007: 158). In the passages from *Lucrece*, Peacham's negative attitude to paradiastole (and the dissembling it stands for) is echoed in the narrator's 'graceless' and 'vile'. And Tarquin's rhetoric is indeed paradiastolary when he redescribes his lust for Lucrece in terms of love, first to himself – 'there is no hate in loving' (240), and 'Love thrives not in the heart that shadows dreadeth' (270) – and later to Lucrece, describing his 'loving tale' (480), and demanding: 'Yield to my love, if not, enforced hate, / Instead of love's coy touch, shall rudely tear thee' (668f.).

The poem uses terms of colouring and cloaking to show how Tarquin hides his intentions in the company of the innocent and unsuspecting Lucrece before the rape. His exterior does not show 'his inward ill' that 'he coloured with his high estate, / Hiding base sin in pleats of majesty; / That nothing in him seemed inordinate' (91–4). Here both colours and the folds of garments ('pleats') are used to portray his deceit, and the naive Lucrece cannot 'pick' any meaning from his 'parling looks, / Nor read the subtle shining secrecies / Writ in the glassy margents of such books' (100–2). In these passages, colours and garments, together with books, margins and failed reading, form a situation of successful rhetorical deception, but one condemned by the narrator.

John Trussell's *Raptus I Helenae. The First Rape of Faire Hellen*, published the year after Shakespeare's *Lucrece*, is heavily influenced by that poem (see Shaaber, 1957: 415–18). That influence also includes a rhetoric of cloaking and colouring. The bulk of the poem is narrated by Helen, framed by eight stanzas in the poet's voice. The Helen of Trussell's poem is young, 'eight score moneths' (43), which is 13 years and four months, but suitors are already approaching her to see her famed beauty, and amongst the visitors is Theseus. The Theseus episode exists in a number of early accounts of the Helen myth (Shaaber, 1957: 418–20; Maguire,

2009: 14), but Trussell's version is unusual in that the rape (usually an abduction for safekeeping) is a sexual rape. The 'first rape' of the poem's title thus refers to this rape by Theseus, and not the later abduction by Paris.

Like Tarquin, Theseus displays a paradiastolary attitude. 'Oft nam'd he love, but then he thought of lust, / oft nam'd he fancy, meaning lechery' (109f.), Helen tells us, and she goes on to explain that she is too innocent to correctly understand Theseus: 'Yet I not knowing lust, too yoong to love, / Could neither fancie nor affection proove' (113f.). Understanding that Helen is not interested, Theseus hides his intentions, and in this section of the poem we find the same terminology we saw used about Tarquin. 'So cunningly he cloked his desire' that Helen believes he has changed his mind (129f.), and when he catches Helen alone on the beach where the rape will take place, again, until the very moment 'his sparks of hidden fire' break forth, he 'did it while then so slylie cloake, / That there might be perceived, nor flame, nor smoke' (148f.). Just like Tarquin, Theseus is successful in his self-representation, cunningly and slyly cloaking his desire and evil intent, and Helen's adverbs signal how we should read this specific instance of cloaking.

Another rapist who figures in the poem is Jove, who famously approached Leda (Helen's mother) in the guise of a swan. Here the cloaking imagery recurs, as 'this Swans shape that shrouded Deity' is termed 'but a shift to cloke impiety' (617f.). Here too the cloaking serves to hide intentions before the act, which Jove carries out in 'his pristine shape', the disguise thrown off: 'For though he counter-feits a feathered weed, / In his owne shape he doth the devillish deed' (628–30). 'Weed' is defined by the *OED* as 'a garment', or 'clothing, apparel' (*OED* 1.a., 2). In this instance too, the narrator (at this point Lerna, Leda's nurse) signals a condemnation of the behaviour.

In the cases of Tarquin, Theseus and Jove, the concepts of cloaking and colouring thus have negative connotations. However, at the end of *Lucrece*, after the suicide but before her father and husband have gathered their wits, Brutus feels obliged to help the situation by doffing his disguise as a fool and urging the men to action. Here we find similar imagery, now employed about one of the heroes of the poem: 'But now he throws that shallow habit by, / Wherein deep policy did him disguise, / And armed his long-hid wits advisedly' (1814–16). As Roe glosses, 'habit' could mean both manner and costume (Roe, 2006: note to line 1814), and we hear echoes of both in the line. Heather Dubrow is right in pointing to the ambiguity surrounding Brutus; like Tarquin, he has mis-led others through his deception (Dubrow, 1987: 126–30). Still, the narratorial comment is positive ('advisedly'), and Brutus' example of cloaking imagery points to the importance of (moral) intention for how colouring and cloaking are represented. This reflects contemporary discussions on the more general topic of lying, as described by for instance Snyder: lying should be avoided but can be accepted when the end is honest, 'honest dissimilation' (Snyder, 2009: 34f., 39f.). Tarquin, Theseus, Jove and Brutus all exemplify rhetorically success-ful instances of cloaking or dissembling – they achieve what they want – but their intentions are important for how their actions are described by the narrative voice in the respective poems.

Lucrece

When we turn to the female characters, we find colouring and cloaking used by and about Lucrece and Helen too. For both heroines, successful rhetorical self-representation is crucial. Lucrece must at the end of the poem convince her husband, Collatine, that she is an innocent victim of rape, and Helen must convince her future husband, Menelaus, that she is a worthy bride. These women are portrayed differently from the men discussed in the previous section, as they start out as unskilled in and innocent of rhetorical representation, and learn the art as their stories progress. Together with the heroines' just complaint, this innocence operates in tension with the distrust of rhetoric displayed by both texts.

A potential problem in a situation with a rhetorically skilled female speaker has been described thus by Anthony Mortimer: 'Since the formal study of rhetoric was seen as a preparation for that public life from which women were excluded, the problem facing the male poet was how to create a genuinely expressive female voice without granting women the rhetorical competence reserved for men' (Mortimer, 2000: 133). Added to this is the more general problem noted above of rhetorical skill as something inherently ambiguous, and to which Lucrece gives voice repeatedly in the poem. However, Shakespeare seems to negotiate these problems through a number of strategies. First of all, he presents Lucrece as innocent and virtuous. Roe draws attention to how Lucrece is described in terms of 'artlessness and simple good faith', 'unsuspecting honesty' and 'uncomplicated virtue' in the early stages of the story, since anything else 'would cloud our impression' (Roe, 2006: 28; Dubrow similarly talks of Lucrece's 'virginal' state [1987: 92]). This innocence includes rhetorical (self-)representation, as 'Lucrece is incapable of discerning the difference between the inward and the outward because she does not perceive this distinction in herself' (Greenstadt, 2010: 64). Lucrece thus fits Quintilian's description of the uneducated and naive reader as someone who can be deceived by rhetorical skill, unlike those trained in the art (Hadfield, 2013: 139).

With the rape, as several critics have pointed out, this changes: 'Thou art not what thou seem'st' (600), Lucrece bursts out in her debate with Tarquin, suddenly aware of duplicity. But she also realises her own *inability* to seem other than she is. She thinks herself transparent, as she has never 'practised how / To cloak offences with a cunning brow' (749), and even the 'illiterate' will be able to read her 'loathsome trespass' by looking at her (810–12). This expressed inability to hide her experience, after she has gained knowledge of duplicity, is another element that distances her from the taint of rhetorical dissimulation. Her notoriously high-strung apostrophes to Night, Opportunity and Time after the rape, together with her address to Philomela (the nightingale and Ovid's rape victim), and her study of the Troy tapestry that hangs in her room, have all been read as rhetorical exercises preparing Lucrece for her final speech to her husband and his followers at the end of the poem (Enterline, 2000; Ellis, 2003; Greenstadt, 2010; Weaver, 2012).[4] William P. Weaver reads this speech in terms of 'forensic performance' against the background of the 'first exercises' of the *progymnasmata* of the grammar school education (Weaver, 2012: Ch. 5), and Amy Greenstadt describes Lucrece's practice and learning process in terms of 'creative' or 'aesthetic imitation' that helps her find her voice and learn how to express grief in line with educational and rhetorical practices of the day (Greenstadt, 2010: 64, 67–70). I want to stress how this education of the initially innocent Lucrece is described as taking place *intuitively* in the poem, as she moves from one thing to another in her room and learns from that situation, starting with her emotional reaction in the night, to the bird at break of dawn, to her meeting with her maid and groom, to her study of the Troy piece. Her learning development may follow that described in rhetorical manuals and schoolbooks, but the poem depicts the situations as naturally occurring, again distancing Lucrece from a planned rhetorical venture. Throughout, Tarquin's sly cloaking hovers as a contrast in the reader's mind.

Weaver points out that the Troy scene develops towards a 'troubled scepticism about representation', as Lucrece once again discovers that 'words and looks can be borrowed for the sake of deception'. As Weaver notes, this goes against her character, and she is shown as 'becoming increasingly impatient with rhetorical exercises as a means of defence' in the second half of the poem (2012: 139). She may learn more and more about rhetorical self-representation, but her disdain for 'idle words, servants to shallow fools' makes her discard them as suitable for 'skill-contending schools' but not able to help her, whose 'case is past the help of law' (1016, 1018, 1021). This is when she decides to take her life (1028f.). The repeatedly verbalised suspicion nevertheless places Lucrece in a tradition of anti-rhetorical rhetoric that goes back to classical Athens, where one way to meet distrust of rhetoric was for the forensic orator to represent himself as rhetorically unskilled or inexperienced, facing a skilled and deceptive opponent (Ober, 1989: 170–7; Hesk, 2000: 208–9). Shakespeare's strategy to portray Lucrece as beyond duplicity by stressing her rhetorical innocence is itself a well-tried move.

Unlike Tarquin, Lucrece will not condescend to paradiastolary embellishment by colouring over what has happened: 'My sable ground of sin I will not paint, / To hide the truth of this false night's abuses' (1074f.). Instead she will 'utter all' and make use of her tears 'to purge [her] impure tale' (1076, 1078). She therefore 'hoards' her passions to use when Collatine arrives, 'When sighs and groans and tears may grace the fashion / Of her disgrace, the better so to clear her / From that suspicion which the world might bear her' (1318–21; cf. Dubrow, 1987: 91). As Weaver notes, '[i]t was a commonplace of classical rhetoric that in order to make an audience weep, the orator had to first feel sorrow' (Weaver, 2012: 138). In Quintilian's words: 'Will [the judge] shed tears if the pleader's eyes are dry? It is utterly impossible' (qtd by Vickers, 1989: 79). Again, Lucrece employs a well-known rhetorical strategy. The question is how far this insight affects the depiction of Lucrece as orator. Perhaps Collatine's surprise at Lucrece's unusual presentation signals a failure as well as a successful rhetorical display, as he obviously notices her sorrow as something put on: 'Why art thou thus attired in discontent? / Unmask, dear dear, this moody heaviness' (1601f.). The cloaking imagery here seems to signal a misfit, a gap between Lucrece and her display of hoarded tears.

Lucrece does unmask her grief, in the sense of telling what has happened, before taking her life. Greenstadt reads Lucrece's suicide as 'part of a greater physical and vocal performance that will attest to her innocence' (Greenstadt, 2010: 67), while Weaver, to my mind correctly, stresses that her suicide 'is described as an alternative to rhetorical representation' and thus constitutes a turn away from rhetoric (Weaver, 2012: 125). Her suicide functions to put an end to rhetorical duplicity, forming an escape from the division Tarquin has forced upon her.

Helen, Menelaus

Like Lucrece, Trussell's Helen is schooled in the art of self-representation over the run of the poem, but unlike that of Lucrece, Helen's self-representation is largely non-verbal; instead it is focused on a cosmetic restoration of beauty. In its tangible use of cloaking and, especially, colouring, Trussell's poem presents Helen as an embodiment of rhetorical embellishment, and thus exploits contemporary discourses about rhetorical as well as cosmetic embellishment.

Helen of Troy is the most famous beauty of Western literature, and one of its most notorious breakers of the marriage bond. As Laurie Maguire notes, in the early modern period 'Helen' was shorthand for a sexually wanton woman or infidelity (Maguire, 2009: 92, 104), and Marina Warner catches some of Helen's impact by describing her arrival in a story as 'almost always carr[ying] that shiver of dread, a foreknowledge that her presence augurs catastrophic consequences, regardless of what she wants or does' (Warner, 2010: n.p.). Norman Austin similarly states that 'Helen was and remains the major scandal' of the Trojan War: 'In the post-Homeric literary tradition Helen is again and again reviled, whether as the treacherous wife or the libertine who preferred pleasure to honor' (Austin, 1994: 1f.). Not very surprisingly, then, like Lucrece's story, Helen's was used to argue *pro et contra* as a school test of debating skill (Maguire, 2009: 94, 83; Weaver, 2012: 137). At the same time, Maguire observes that in both the classical and the early modern periods, there is a doubleness in attitude towards Helen: she is represented as more or less worthy of blame in different accounts (2009: 129, 139, and Ch. 4 *passim*). Classical examples are the encomia of Gorgias and Isocrates, who 'accepted the traditional Helen as Homer had represented her, but then presented her case as if they were her counsel defending her in a court of law. These encomia have been interpreted as bravura legal performances, demonstrating the orators' skill at making the worse cause appear the better' (Austin, 1994: 3). Trussell's little-discussed poem on Helen displays such characteristics and tensions: a very young poet's work,[5] the complaint is obsessive in its display of rhetorical skill (most obviously noticeable in its overuse of alliteration). It aligns itself with the two Greek encomia in its portrayal of a Helen deserving to be defended. Yet, Trussell's decision to depict Helen before she became the 'scandal' of the Trojan War, and his other strategies similar to those of Shakespeare, work in tension with a potential for an ambiguous reading of her project of restorative self-representation.

Much like Lucrece, Helen has to learn about the erratic relation between being and seeming, and like Shakespeare's poem, Trussell makes use of cloaking and colouring to describe such situations. After the rape, Helen shuns the sun, believing it will reveal her 'disgrace' (214), and she tries to decide how to act, whether to return to court, whether to tell what has happened or whether to exile herself, seeking the best way to 'cloak' her ruined name (308). Using the same metaphor, upon Helen's return to court, her mother asks her 'not by cloaking it thy sorrow keep', but to tell what has happened in order to ease the pain and let others share her sorrow (457–62). After these instances, cloaking is used expressly in combination with 'secrecy', as Helen is advised to hide what has happened. The two nurses who have overheard Helen's curses of Theseus and the ravishment tell her that her shame is not visible and, moreover, virginity itself is 'cloak'd so close with secrecie' that no one can tell it is lost unless pregnancy gives the woman away (547–52). The advice to Helen is thus to 'Cloake it with secrecy' (576), and this is justified by her refusal and Theseus' use of force (565–8): 'Blamelesse thou art although thou blotted be, / Yet if thou blab not, none this blot can see' (569–70). The nurses offer further support for secrecy in Leda, who 'cloake[d]' Jove's rape with such secrecy that no one was in doubt of her constancy, even though she was impregnated (641–2). We recognise Trussell's strategies from Shakespeare's poem: Helen's youth and innocence, Theseus' use of force and the fact that she has to be taught self-representation all contribute to a positive portrait, distancing Helen from the taint of 'cloaking'.

'Decrease thy sorrow and increase thy beautie' (726), her mother tells her, and the instances of cloaking give way to colouring as the work to restore Helen's beauty begins. This restoration can be seen as a rhetorical process, with Helen putting on, applying, the rhetorical self. A stock component of the complaints, beauty is often linked to rhetoric, as in Daniel's *Rosamond*, where beauty is described as 'Dombe eloquence, whose powre doth move the blood, / More then the words, or wisdome of the wise' (Daniel, 1930: 122f.). In Shakespeare's complaint, Tarquin uses it to excuse his rape: 'All orators are dumb when beauty pleadeth' (267). But in the case of Helen the power of beauty goes beyond this, as Austin reminds us: 'whoever possessed beauty in Homeric society would possess the world, so high was the value placed on beauty' (Austin, 1994: 24). For Helen, at least in Trussell's poem, beauty is the one means to affect her situation, and in this way, too, comparable to Lucrece's use of rhetoric.

After the women's joint persuasions, Helen discards her sorrow 'And only studied how to get that collour, / which melancholy had exiled hence' (765f.). The makeover is described in (for the time) unusually positive terms:

> Looke what by Arte, or nature could be thought,
> powerfull to polish my late perish'd plumes.
> Was neither left unvalued, nor unbought.
> till what by diets, paintings, and perfumes,
> My beautie of her blemish was deprived,
> And my so late-collour [*sic*] was revived.[6]

(769–74)

Trussell had precedent for his positive account of cosmetic restoration. In *Ars Amatoria*, Ovid looks positively on the use of make-up, but the process and the materials should be kept hidden from the lover: 'let no lover find the boxes set upon the table; your looks are aided by dissembled art' ('*ars faciem dissimulata iuvat*') (Ovid, 1962: 132f.). Karim-Cooper takes this to suggest 'that it is their deception or artifice to which potential suitors are attracted' (2006: 111, 125), but the phrasing in Ovid seems to indicate that it is because of the dissembling the products need to be kept hidden. Of special relevance to Helen's situation is Ovid's admonition to hide blemishes, faults and flaws (1962: 137, 139), which would justify her cosmetic restoration.

Still, as Karim-Cooper has shown, cosmetic painting in the early modern period was a complex matter, described in the harshest terms in anti-cosmetic tracts, at the same time as manuals and recipe books obviously catered to an existing market, and make-up was employed on the public stages. In the complaints, the heroines are always described as naturally beautiful, sometimes in contrast to made-up women. Daniel's Rosamond distances herself from cosmetics in the strongest terms, likening make-up to 'borrowed blush which banck-rot beauties seeke' and speaking of 'Th'adulterate beauty of a falsed cheeke: / Vild staine to honor and to women eeke', moving through impiety, falsehood, treason, and ending up likening make-up to idolatry (Daniel, 1930: 134–47), all standard associations at the time (Karim-Cooper, 2006: 34–49). Richard Barnfield published a nine-stanza diatribe against cosmetics in reply to Michael Drayton's *Matilda*, 'The Complaint of Chastitie' (1595). It should be noted that one factor such accusations have in common with suspicions levelled at rhetorical display is the idea of deception, of a beautiful surface hiding something else.

Against this context, it is only to be expected that Trussell's poem too can be taken to imply more ambiguous readings of Helen's cosmetic transformation. Most obviously, this happens in the peacock imagery employed in three stanzas following the one discussed above:

> Then as the wearer of poore *Argus* eies,
>   doth vaunt his proud plumes in his majestie:
> Yet when his Prides ill-pleasing legges he spies,
>   he falls his plumes, and vailes his royaltie.
> Shaming as seems, his plumes with collours graced,
> Should be with such disgracing legges defaced.
>
> So did I flaunt in new-found fond disguise,
>   (such as at this day court attenders weare:
> When with newfangles they Idolatrize
>   the banckrout beautie of their borrowed haire.)
> Such did I weare, although I needed none,
> My beauty lackt no blazon but her owne.
>
> Yet when I thought I was in highest pleasure,
>   and my thoughts pleasure in the highest rate:
> If I but thought of my so late lost treasure,
>   it would my present pleasure so amate,
> That as the Peacoks legs doe bate his pride,
> So do my losse my lives contentment hide.
>
> (775–92)

John Aylmer, Bishop of London, claimed that the plain style of dress Elizabeth I adopted in her youth made court ladies 'ashamed to be dressed and painted like peacocks' (qtd by Karim-Cooper, 2006: 62), indicating that the peacock was associated with gaudy dress and make-up. In the passage, Helen contrasts herself specifically with courtiers, stressing that unlike them she does not normally need any of the products and materials she now uses, since her 'beauty lackt no blazon but her owne'. The term 'blazon' carries the sense of poetic description of a woman's beauty, supporting a reading of the beautifying process in terms of rhetorical embellishment. But the heraldic term also carries overtones of both (descriptive) display and shielding (*OED* n. I, II), as shown by Helen's juxtaposition of 'flaunt[ing]' and 'disguise'. The complex, or ambiguous, interconnection of display and shield can be understood in a military context. Maguire writes about make-up as 'arming' when discussing the episode from the *Iliad* in which Hera seduces Zeus, where it is not her 'essential' beauty but her beauty as 'prosthetic' that is described: 'In a military epic, this is a scene of *female* arming [...] Women's armour is beauty; beauty is something we can put on' (Maguire, 2009: 74; emphasis original). Similarly, what goes on in Trussell can be read in terms of restoration and prostheticising, preparation and arming. In a universe where Jove habitually steps down to ravish whoever is available at the same time as virtue and beauty are the highest female qualities, such arming seems justified. Further, the interconnection of display and shield, and the military sphere of reference, is inherent in the rhetorical concept of *ornatus*, familiar to early modern rhetoricians, where the military sense of being equipped for war is transferred to rhetorical ornament: 'To be properly *ornatus* is to be equipped for battle, powerfully armoured and protected. What the rhetoricians are claiming is that "ornaments" characteristic of the Grand Style are not mere decorations and embellishments; they are the weapons an orator must learn to wield' (Skinner, 1996: 49). In its complex associations, the passage in Trussell's poem thus invites an understanding of cosmetic (or rhetorical) embellishment as protection, display *as* shield.

The passage further refers to the peacock's proverbial pride, and specifically the ugliness of the peacock's legs. Drayton too likens King John's inability to gain Matilda's love to the peacock's shame 'when his Lead-pale legs hee haps to see' (Drayton, 1961: 676), and the image goes back at least as far as the *Physiologus* (second century AD, often attributed to Epiphanius of Salamis) with its descriptions and moral readings of animals.[7] Of the peacock it says that it is the proudest bird, and very beautiful, but when it beholds its legs it cries out loud, since they do not match the rest of its body ('*cum autem suos conspicit pedes suos graviter vociferatur, scilicet quod illi caeteris corporis sui partibus non respondeant*'). The moral reading is that 'the worldly man will cry out to God when he sees the ugliness of his sin', the feet figuring the sin ('*Pedes, id est, peccata*') (*Physiologus*, 1588: 48f.; Badke, 2004: 'Peacock'). When Helen mentions the peacock's legs, the potential for an ambiguous reading of the makeover episode definitely enters the poem, as her lost chastity is described in ways that associate it with sin. Similarly, the description of Menelaus in terms of a 'cloake' and a 'foile' for Helen at the end of the poem creates tension as it plays into contemporary anti-cosmetic attitudes (860, 875). 'Sexual entrapment is one of the chief accusations polemicists level at painted women', according to Karim-Cooper (2006: 46), and marriage is, after all, the ultimate motive for Helen's cosmetic restoration (719f.).

At the same time, despite an inequality in awareness, the couple is portrayed as happy at the end of Helen's tale. Perhaps, in Trussell's poem cosmetics can be seen to function in a similar way as Karim-Cooper claims they do in Thomas Middleton's *The Revenger's Tragedy* (1607) and *The Second Maiden's Tragedy* (1611), where cosmetic paint 'becomes a cleansing agent for the political body', acting as a purgative for 'sexual sin' of the tyrant and the court (Karim-Cooper, 2006: 67, 69 and Ch. 3 *passim*). Towards the end of the poem Helen describes her rape as 'covered, ended, and cleane extirpate' (878), that is, 'rooted out, destroyed utterly, rendered extinct' (*OED*, †extirpate, *adj.*).

Conclusion

Shakespeare and Trussell set themselves highly challenging rhetorical tasks when choosing the stories of Lucrece and Helen for their respective complaints, and the many instances of colouring and cloaking found in the poems – favourite metaphors of early modern rhetoricians to describe their art – signal the poets' awareness of this challenge. As we have seen, the poets employ a number of strategies to set up a contrast between unacceptable and acceptable versions of rhetorical dissimulation: paradiastole and cloaking imagery together with narratorial commentary mark the rapists' rhetorical dissembling as morally despicable, while Lucrece's and Helen's innocence and need for schooling help present their employment of rhetorical and cosmetic strategies of self-representation as defensible. Still, the inescapable ambiguity inherent in an art that employs colouring and cloaking metaphors to describe anything from the 'beautification' of rhetorical embellishment to a paradiastolary disordering of vices and virtues shows through clearly. Lucrece's verbalised rhetorical innocence and hoarding up of tears risk turning on herself, while Helen's embodiment of rhetorical tropes of embellishment illustrates the complexity of rhetorical and cosmetic ornament used for 'flaunting' *and* 'disguise', display *and* shield. One could say that the poets and their heroines are inextricably caught in the web of rhetoric, expanding far beyond these poems to encompass the early modern culture of secrecy, with its inherent suspicions of dishonest dissembling. Or one could say that they play the rhetorical game, their frequent employment of colouring and cloaking signalling their full awareness of the challenges involved. In either case, the peacock's legs will never be completely hidden.

Acknowledgements

I would like to express my gratitude to the editors of this issue of *EJES* for their helpful and very inspiring comments. I would also like to thank Hans Helander for initial discussions about paradiastole.

Disclosure statement

No potential conflict of interest was reported by the author.

Notes

1. When using old-spelling editions I have regularised u and v, i and j, and s in the quotations.
2. In the complaints group I include: Samuel Daniel's *The Complaint of Rosamond* (1592), Thomas Churchyard's revised *Shores Wife* (1593), Anthony Chute's *Beautie Dishonoured. Written under the title of Shores Wife* (1593), Thomas Lodge's *The Complaint of Elstred* (1593), William Shakespeare's *Lucrece* (1594), Michael Drayton's *Matilda* (1594), Richard Barnfield's *Cassandra* (1595), John Trussell's *Raptus I Helenae. The First Rape of Faire Hellen* (1595) and Thomas Middleton's *The Ghost of Lucrece* (1600). See Swärdh (2011) for a description of the group.
3. 'Cloak' carries meanings of concealment and pretence (*OED* n. 3.a.; v. 2.b., 3, 2014), while 'colour' is used to refer to rhetorical figures and embellishment (*OED* n. II. 15; v. II. 5), to outward appearance and to representing something either in a false or positive light (*OED* n. II. 7; v. II. 6).
4. Weaver and Greenstadt have published articles containing essentially the same material as the relevant chapters in their monographs (Weaver, 2008; Greenstadt, 2006). I refer only to the monographs in my parenthetical references, but list the articles in the bibliography.
5. John Trussell (*c.*1575–1648) wrote historiographical and antiquarian works besides a few poems, including three dedicatory verses to Robert Southwell's *Triumphs over Death* (Shaaber, 1957: 407–18; Rosen, 2008).
6. Line 774 does not scan easily in Shaaber's edition, and 'late-lost collour' would make more sense and add a missing syllable. I have not seen the 1595 text.
7. I am indebted to Gordon Campbell for directing me to the *Physiologus*.

References

Austin, Norman (1994). *Helen of Troy and Her Shameless Phantom*. Ithaca, NY: Cornell UP.

Badke, Davis (2004). Commentary and transcript. *Physiologus* (1588). Plantin ed. Accessed 4 March 2014. http://spcoll.library.uvic.ca/Digit/physiologum/index.html.

Barnfield, Richard (1990a). 'Cassandra.' [1595]. *Richard Barnfield: The Complete Poems*. Ed. George Klawitter. Selinsgrove: Susquehanna UP.

Barnfield, Richard (1990b). 'The Complaint of Chastitie.' [1595]. *Richard Barnfield: The Complete Poems*. Ed. George Klawitter. Selinsgrove: Susquehanna UP.

Castiglione, Baldesar [Baldassare] (1967). *The Book of the Courtier*. Trans. and introd. George Bull. Penguin Classics. London: Penguin.

Churchyard, Thomas (1593). *The Tragedie of Shores Wife, Churchyards Challenge*. London: John Wolfe. STC 522099.

Chute, Anthony (1593). *Beautie Dishonoured Written under the Title of Shores Wife*. London: John Wolfe. STC 5262.

Coignet, Mathieu [Martin] (1586). *A Politic Discourse upon Truth and Lying [...]*. London: Ralphe Newberie. STC 5486.

Daniel, Samuel (1930). 'The Complaint of Rosamond.' [1592]. *Poems and a Defence of Ryme*. Ed. Arthur Colby Sprague. Cambridge, MA: Harvard UP.

Day, Angel (1586; augmented 1592). *The English Secretorie*. London: Robert Waldegrave. STC 6401; STC 6402.

Drayton, Michael (1961). 'Matilda. The Faire and Chaste Daughter of the Lord Robert Fitzwater.' [1594]. *The Works of Michael Drayton*. Vol. 1. Ed. J. William Hebel. 6 vols. Oxford: Shakespeare Head Press.

Dubrow, Heather (1987). *Captive Victors: Shakespeare's Narrative Poems and Sonnets*. Ithaca, NY: Cornell UP.

Ellis, Jim (2003). *Sexuality and Citizenship: Metamorphosis in Elizabethan Erotic Verse*. Toronto: U of Toronto P.

Enterline, Lynn (2000). *The Rhetoric of the Body from Ovid to Shakespeare*. Cambridge: Cambridge UP.

Greenstadt, Amy (2010). *Rape and the Rise of the Author: Gendering Intention in Early Modern England*. Farnham: Ashgate.

Greenstadt, Amy (2006). '"Read It in Me": The Author's Will in *Lucrece*.' *Shakespeare Quarterly* 57.1: 45–70.

Hadfield, Andrew (2013). 'Literature and the Culture of Lying before the Enlightenment.' *Studia Neophilologica* 85.2: 133–47.

Hesk, Jon (2000). *Deception and Democracy in Classical Athens*. Cambridge: Cambridge UP.

Karim-Cooper, Farah (2006). *Cosmetics in Shakespeare and Renaissance Drama*. Edinburgh: Edinburgh UP.

Lodge, Thomas (1593). *Phillis: Honoured with Pastorall Sonnets, Elegies, and Amorous Delights. Where-unto is Annexed, the Tragicall Complaynt of Elstred*. London: John Busbie. STC 16662.

Maguire, Laurie (2009). *Helen of Troy: From Homer to Hollywood*. Chichester: Wiley-Blackwell.

Middleton, Thomas (1937). *The Ghost of Lucrece*. [1600]. Eds Adams Joseph Quincy. Folger Shakespeare Library Publications. New York: Charles Scribner's Sons.

Mortimer, Anthony (2000). *Variable Passions: A Reading of Shakespeare's 'Venus and Adonis'*. New York: AMS Press.

Ober, Josiah (1989). *Mass and Elite in Democratic Athens: Rhetoric, Ideology, and the Power of the People*. Princeton, NJ: Princeton UP.

OED. Oxford English Dictionary Online (2014). Oxford: Oxford UP.

Ovid (1962). *The Art of Love, and Other Poems*. Trans. J.H. Mozley. Loeb Classical Library. Cambridge, MA: Harvard UP.

Peacham, Henry (1577; 1593). *The Garden of Eloquence*. London: H. Jackson. STC 19498; STC 19497.

Physiologus (1588). Plantin ed. Accessed 4 March 2014. http://spcoll.library.uvic.ca/Digit/physiologum/index.html

Puttenham, George (2007). *The Art of English Poesy*. [1588]. Ed. Frank Whigham and Wayne A. Rebhorn. Ithaca, NY: Cornell UP. *Physiologus*. Plantin ed. Accessed 4 March 2014. http://spcoll.library.uvic.ca/Digit/physiologum/index.html.

Roe, John, ed. (2006). *The Poems: Venus and Adonis, The Rape of Lucrece, The Phoenix and the Turtle, The Passionate Pilgrim, A Lover's Complaint*. [1992]. New Cambridge Shakespeare. Cambridge: Cambridge UP.

Rosen, Adrienn (2008). 'Trussell, John (bap. 1575, d. 1648).' *Oxford Dictionary of National Biography*. Oxford: Oxford UP. 2004. Online ed. Accessed 17 May 2015. http://www.oxforddnb.com.ezp.sub.su.se/view/article/27778?docPos=2.

Shaaber, M.A., ed. (1957). 'The First Rape of Faire Hellen by John Trussell.' *Shakespeare Quarterly* 8: 407–45.

Shakespeare, William (2003). *Hamlet, Prince of Denmark. The Complete Works of Shakespeare.* Ed. David Bevington. New York: Longman.

Shakespeare, William (2006). *The Rape of Lucrece. [1594] The Poems: Venus and Adonis, The Rape of Lucrece, The Phoenix and the Turtle, The Passionate Pilgrim, A Lover's Complaint.* Ed. John Roe. [1992]. New Cambridge Shakespeare. Cambridge: Cambridge UP. Updated ed.

Skinner, Quentin (2007). 'Paradiastole: Redescribing the Vices as Virtues.' *Renaissance Figures of Speech.* Eds AdamsonSylvia, Gavin Alexander and Katrin Ettenhuber. Cambridge: Cambridge UP. 149–63.

Skinner, Quentin (1996). *Reason and Rhetoric in the Philosophy of Hobbes.* Cambridge: Cambridge UP.

Snyder, Jon (2009). *Dissimulation and the Culture of Secrecy in Early Modern Europe.* Berkeley: U of California P.

Swärdh, Anna (2011). 'Elizabethan Complaints.' *The Literary Encyclopedia.* <http://litencyc.com>.

Trussell, John (1957). 'Raptus I Helenae. The First Rape of Faire Hellen.' [1595]. *The First Rape of Faire Hellen by John Trussell.* Ed. M.A. Shaaber. *Shakespeare Quarterly* 8: 421–45.

Vickers, Brian, ed. (1999). *English Renaissance Literary Criticism.* Oxford: Clarendon.

Vickers, Brian (1989). *In Defence of Rhetoric.* [1988]. Oxford: Clarendon.

Warner, Marina (2010). 'Did She Go Willingly?: Helen of Troy.' Review of Laurie Maguire's *Helen of Troy: From Homer to Hollywood. London Review of Books* 32.19: 24–26. Accessed 31 March 2014. http://www.lrb.co.uk/v32/n19/marina-warner/did-she-go-willingly.

Weaver, William P. (2008). '"O teach me how to make mine own excuse": Forensic Performance in *Lucrece.*' *Shakespeare Quarterly* 59.4: 421–49.

Weaver, William P. (2012). *Untutored Lines: The Making of The English Epyllion.* Edinburgh, Scotland: Edinburgh UP.

Whigham, Frank and Rebhorn, Wayne A., eds (2007). *The Art of English Poesy. By George Puttenham.* Ithaca: Cornell UP.

Wilson, Thomas (1999). 'The Arte of Rhetorique [1553].' *English Renaissance Literary Criticism.* Ed. Brian Vickers. Oxford: Clarendon.

Zagorin, Perez (1990). *Ways of Lying: Dissimulation, Persecution, and Conformity in Early Modern Europe.* Cambridge, MA: Harvard UP.

Anna Swärdh is a senior lecturer in English literature at Karlstad University, Sweden. Her dissertation *Rape and Religion in English Renaissance Literature* (Uppsala, 2003) studied a number of literary texts against the background of religious controversies in the wake of the English Reformation. She went on to study formal and generic aspects of late Elizabethan complaint poetry in a project sponsored by the Swedish Research Council, 'The Emulative Complaint'. She has also published on historical and contemporary adaptations and productions of Shakespeare.

Eric Pudney

MENDACITY AND KINGSHIP IN SHAKESPEARE'S *HENRY V* AND *RICHARD III*

Shakespeare's Henry V and Richard III both practise mendacity, but while Henry V *celebrates Henry's capacity for deceit, the king's lies are condemned in* Richard III. *The plays show how similar patterns of behaviour in early modern England could be represented as either virtuous or evil by means of rhetoric, while the similar behaviour of the two kings suggests a broad awareness of the necessity of deceit as a political skill. These two plays also draw attention to their own rhetorical distortions in ways which have appeared troubling to many modern critics, but which exemplify humanist ideas about education through rhetorical 'lies'.*

... least the good should be confused and so confounded with the bad; or that we should under the name of a tyrant comprehend them also which were right worthy and famous men: let vs compare the worst tyrant with the best king.

(Bodin, 1606: 211)

Shakespeare's two best-known English kings – Henry V and Richard III – have traditionally been regarded as opposites (Tillyard, 1944: 309; Ribner, 1957: 182), but in fact they have a good deal in common – particularly in terms of their use of mendacity. While the deceptive acts they perpetrate in order to maintain a hold on power are very differently presented – to be approved of in Henry and condemned in Richard – the similarities between them are perhaps even more striking than the differences. Henry and Richard are examples of the best possible and the worst imaginable kings, but they both practise deceit. In fact, the only king in the two tetralogies of history plays with nothing to hide and no aptitude for deceit is Henry VI. His reign, not coincidentally, is disastrous.[1]

These observations sit uneasily with what was the most commonly expressed view of mendacity during the early modern period: that it was a vice of which no Christian – let alone a king – should be guilty. Lying was widely condemned by humanist authors such as Erasmus, who associates it with tyranny (1936: 163) and, in England, Sir Thomas Elyot. Most of these writers – the most famous exception being Machiavelli – would have agreed that any moral shortcoming was bad in ordinary people, but even worse in kings, whose exalted position demanded correspondingly great virtues. By this logic, a prince ought to avoid the vice of lying at all costs.

This view of the matter is summarised by Elyot in *The Boke Named the Gouernour* (1531), one of a number of works from the period which sought to outline the correct means of educating a future ruler in order to ensure a virtuous reign. Elyot considers which vice is the worse, violence or mendacity:

> fraude semeth to be proprely of the foxe, violence or force of the lyon, the one and the other be farre from the nature of man, but fraude is worthy moste to be hated. That maner of iniurie, whiche is done with fraude and disceyte, is at this present tyme so communely practised, that if it be but a litle, it is called policie, and if it be moche and with a visage of grauitie, it is than named and accounted for wisedome.

> (Elyot, 1531: III, 110)

'Fraude', then, is more hateful – and unnatural – than violence. Elyot deplores it, while ruefully admitting that it is widespread. He also indicates that fraud is rarely designated as such. What is deceit to Elyot may be seen as wisdom from somebody else's perspective. The designation of a vice as a virtue, or of a virtue as a vice, is known in rhetoric as *paradiastole*. The abuse of *paradiastole* had long been associated with the court by the time Shakespeare wrote; Wyatt's poetry made this connection in the 1530s (Skinner, 2002: 278–9; see also the essay by Anna Swärdh in the present issue).

This article argues that deceit was widely, albeit usually tacitly, understood to be part of a king's job in early modern England – both in Shakespeare's plays and in other writings. While some, such as Elyot, may have deplored this state of affairs, almost everybody connected with the court would have accepted it to be the case. Furthermore, in a political culture well versed in rhetoric, it was always possible to describe any action as either virtuous or vicious, depending on the demands of expediency. Mendacity was no exception; it could be represented either as unspeakable evil or as laudable wisdom. An example of each possibility is provided in the title characters of *Richard III* and *Henry V*.

The evil characters in *Richard III*, as might be expected, are liars. Richard himself, 'hell's black intelligencer', hardly lets a scene go by without telling an untruth. Richard is frequently able to trick the other characters, over whom he exercises verbal dominance. However, as a recent editor of the play points out, he is rarely able to conceal his basic villainy from them (Siemon, 2009: 7). Another feature of his character is his occasional failure to persuade. He cannot convince Buckingham to help him murder the princes, and is forced to rely on Tyrrel, who requires a cash payment. He is also unable to persuade Hastings to support his claim to the throne, despite his apparent belief that this will be an 'easy matter' (3.1.161) and the fact that he wins Hastings' goodwill by executing several of his enemies.

The play's supporting villain, Buckingham, is also a skilful liar who claims he can 'counterfeit the deep tragedian', and has both 'ghastly looks' and 'enforced smiles' at his service (3.5.5–9). Buckingham easily tricks the Lord Mayor, by lying to him, into justifying the execution of Hastings to the citizens of London. Strangely for such a skilled deceiver, however, Buckingham fails to persuade the citizens of London to accept Richard as their king. He recounts his rhetorical efforts to present Richard in an appealing light, as a ruler with 'discipline in war, wisdom in peace … bounty, virtue, [and] fair humility' (3.7.16–17).

Interestingly, many of these statements are *not* exactly lies; for the most part they are an attempt to represent Richard as a competent ruler by means of rhetoric. There is a case to be made along these lines; Richard certainly takes effective steps to consolidate his hold on power, and there are lines in the play which support Buckingham's claims, certainly as far as Richard's 'discipline in war' is concerned.[2] Nonetheless, the citizens are completely unmoved; they respond 'like dumb statues or breathing stones' (3.7.25). Despite his skills as a liar (or perhaps precisely because of them), Buckingham is a failure as a rhetorician: he can trick, lie and deceive, but oratory and persuasion are beyond him.

Buckingham's response to his failure is characteristic of his and Richard's tactics. The Recorder is asked to speak to the people, and

> When he had done, some followers of mine own
> At lower end of the hall hurled up their caps,
> And some ten voices cried, 'God save King Richard!'
> And thus I took the vantage of those few:
> 'Thanks, gentle citizens and friends,' quoth I;
> 'This general applause and cheerful shout
> Argues your wisdom and your love to Richard'
>
> (3.7.34–40)

The only way in which Buckingham can respond to his failed attempt at oratory is to resort to an act of deception. Both his trickery and his rhetorical incompetence set him apart from the good characters.

The association between the good characters and rhetoric is established in a scene which mirrors Richard's earlier discussion of lying with Buckingham. Elizabeth, wanting revenge against Richard, asks Margaret to teach her how to curse. Margaret tells her:

> Think that thy babes were sweeter than they were,
> And he that slew them fouler than he is.
> Bettering thy loss makes the bad causer worse.
> Revolving this will teach thee how to curse.
>
> (4.4.120–3)

Curses are expressed in words, and this advice is similar to that of early modern rhetorical manuals on how to make words powerful. Margaret urges Elizabeth to employ the rhetorical technique of amplification: exaggerating virtue and vice in ways which are convenient to the purpose she sets out to achieve. This is one of the most important rhetorical tools, according to the rhetorician Thomas Wilson: 'Among all the figures of Rhetorique, there is no one that so muche helpeth forward an oration' (1580: 118). Amplification is simply a way of 'augmentyng, and diminishyng of any matter' – colouring the listener's perception of the 'matter' by the way in which it is described. Wilson's examples of this invaluable skill are illuminating: 'When I see one sore beaten, to saie he is slaine: to call a naughtie fellow thief, or hangman, when he is not knowne to bee any suche' (123). Margaret's advice is not quite this concrete, but she suggests that Richard's vices should be exaggerated in a similar manner.

The seemingly straightforward distinction between 'good' rhetoric and 'bad' lying established in the play, then, is much less clear than it first appears. Both lying and rhetoric, as described by Margaret, involve verbal distortion of the truth, and the involvement of the good characters in the play in a kind of deception complicates the play's black-and-white morality. The advice Margaret gives to Elizabeth raises a particularly awkward issue, by suggesting that the bad might not be as bad as the good choose to imagine them to be. The fact that Richard is rhetorically described as worse than he really is by Elizabeth and Margaret raises the possibility that the play also presents Richard as worse than the historical Richard actually was. *Richard III* hints at the ubiquity of deception as a political tool, complicating the play's depiction of lying as evil and perhaps even undermining its own representation of Richard's villainy. The problem is compounded by the numerous parallels between Richard's behaviour and that of his supposed antithesis, Henry V.

While Richard frequently tells outright lies, Henry's deceptions are much more subtle. An early example is that Henry misleads the French ambassadors as to his reasons for declaring war – glossing over the fact that the decision has already been taken *before* Henry receives the Dauphin's insulting gift of tennis balls. That Henry, as king, can deceive so deftly would be no surprise to members of early modern audiences who had already seen the *Henry IV* plays. In these, Henry, as Prince Hal, trains himself in the dark arts of deception by associating with the incorrigible liar Falstaff. His father regrets this behaviour, but in *2 Henry IV* Warwick gives him credit for it, explaining that '[t]he prince but studies his companions/Like a strange tongue' (4.4.68–9) and correctly predicts that Hal will ultimately reject his low friends.

Apart from 'studying' Falstaff, Hal is already thinking ahead to his future role as king. As he explains in a soliloquy:

> herein will I imitate the sun,
> Who doth permit the base contagious clouds
> To smother up his beauty from the world,
> That, when he please again to be himself,
> Being wanted, he may be more wondered at.
>
> (*1 Henry IV* 1.2.187–91)

Hal pretends to be worse than he really is because by falsely representing himself as dissolute, he can make his eventual transformation into a great king all the more impressive. An analogous pretence is present in *Richard III*: Richard represents himself as better than he really is in order to win the throne, for example when he poses with two bishops in order to impress the Lord Mayor in the third act. His pretended piety is only abandoned at the end of the play when he declares that '[c]onscience is but a word that cowards use' (5.3.309). The behaviour of the two kings-to-be is very similar, even if the audience's expected reaction is very different.

After they have been crowned, both Henry and Richard use trickery against their political enemies. The scene in *Richard III* in which the execution of Hastings is ordered is a deceitful performance on the part of Buckingham and Richard, for the benefit of the rest of the council. When Richard makes his furious accusations of witchcraft against Edward's wife and his mistress Jane Shore, Hastings does not even contradict him, but the word 'if' is enough excuse for Richard to demand his execution: 'If? Thou protector of this damned strumpet, /Talk'st thou to me of ifs? Thou art a traitor. / – Off with his head' (3.4.73–5). The excuse is very obviously fabricated, and the decision to execute Hastings has been made in advance. The treatment of Hastings is an act of tyranny, and this point is reinforced by a scene entirely devoted to the speech of the scrivener who takes care of the paperwork after the event. The pretence of legal process is a 'palpable device' (3.6.11).

In *Henry V*, Henry deals with his three enemies Scroop, Cambridge and Grey in an equally mendacious manner. Henry begins by asking Exeter to pardon 'the man committed yesterday/That railed upon our person' (2.2.40–1). This appears to be a straightforward act of mercy, but it turns out to be a trap into which the traitors obligingly step. Scroop, Cambridge and Grey protest against Henry's excessive lenience and urge him to punish the prisoner. Henry pardons the offender anyway, and then offers the trio their commissions to read – but in fact, the papers he hands them are arrest warrants. When they beg for mercy, Henry is able to retort that '[t]he mercy that was quick in us but late/By your own counsel is suppressed and killed' (2.2.79–80). In this play, the paperwork has been correctly filled out in advance, and the moral orientation of this scene is the reverse of that in Richard's treatment of Hastings. The men really are traitors and everybody approves of their execution; they themselves publicly acknowledge that they deserve to die (2.2.151–65). But despite the emphatic assertion of the justice of Henry's decision, the manner in which the traitors' downfall is engineered involves trickery, just like Richard's handling of Hastings.

As well as using trickery themselves, both Richard and Henry encourage others to engage in mendacity. Buckingham's metatheatrical boasts about his ability to deceive, and his bravura performance in fooling the Lord Mayor, are brought out by Richard's verbal incitement (3.5.1–4). Henry, in his speech before the gates of Harfleur, does not seek to induce real anger in his men but tells them how to fake it (Leggatt, 1988: 130). Henry encourages his troops to 'imitate the action of the tiger' and '[d]isguise fair nature' (3.1.6–8). Both Richard and Henry give their followers lessons in deception.

Both Richard and Henry mistrust their troops, and both kings feel the need to spy on their own men. In Richard's case, his reasons for sneaking around his camp in the night are expressed openly. Richard intends to 'play the eavesdropper, /To see if any mean to shrink from me' (5.3.221–2). In *Henry V*, the king's motivation for disguising himself and talking to his men is not stated explicitly. The chorus suggests that Henry raises morale among his men with 'a little touch of Harry in the night', but as Annabel Patterson points out, this is not borne out by what is shown on stage (1989: 77). It seems more likely that Henry is in disguise in order to get a better idea of the morale of his men, since they will speak more freely in front of him if they do not know who he is.

This impression is strengthened by the fact that Henry engages his men in conversation about the king and their feelings for him. When Bates expresses the wish that Henry were 'here alone', Henry replies, 'I dare say you love him not so ill, to wish him here alone, howsoever you speak this to feel other men's minds' (4.1.121; 124–6). The line is laden with irony, since 'feeling other men's minds' is precisely what Henry, not Bates, is doing. This kind of spying might seem to be an undignified activity for a monarch to engage in, which may explain why Henry's motivation is glossed over and why Richard's intentions are made so clear. But despite the differences in the way the two kings' actions are represented, their activities are very similar, as is their lack of faith in their followers.

Both kings marry for political reasons, and both engage in deceit while wooing their future wives. Richard speaks to Anne in the style of a grovelling Petrarchan lover, but after having won her over – despite considerable doubts on her part which never seem to be resolved – he comments to the audience that 'I'll have her, but I will not keep her long' (1.2.232), further emphasising his villainy and hinting at her eventual murder.

Henry, like Richard, professes love for his wife-to-be, and his performance is much more convincing. But the play makes it abundantly clear that he is marrying Katherine for political reasons. Previously in the play, the chorus reports that Henry has already been offered Katherine's hand in marriage, along with 'a few petty dukedoms'. This offer 'likes not' (3.0.32), so marriage to Katherine cannot be of primary concern for Henry – at least not for its own sake. The peace treaty must be sealed by a marriage, and all concerned are well aware of this before Henry and Katherine have even met; this is why, in an earlier scene, Katherine is shown practising her English. Henry's protestations of love are of questionable sincerity, and the suspicion that Henry's speech is an example of rhetoric rather than open-hearted sincerity is strengthened by the fact that Henry represents himself to Katherine as a poor speaker, with 'neither words nor measure' (5.2.135). This claim, from the perspective of an audience that has seen France conquered largely by Henry's rousing speeches, cannot be taken at face value.

The suggestion that kings are always deceivers might seem to be problematic, and many modern critics have concluded that Henry is far from being the perfect hero he has traditionally been thought (a recent example is Fitter, 2002). How could early modern audiences accept Henry, a deceiver, as a hero? It has already been remarked that Thomas Elyot, among many others, condemned 'fraude', but this was not the only opinion on the question. The most famous rejection of the moralistic view is set out in Machiavelli's *The Prince* (1532), which was available in manuscript translation in England from the 1580s (Sharpe, 2009: 463). Machiavelli's view of mendacity is entirely pragmatic:

Everyone realises how praiseworthy it is for a prince to honour his word and to be straightforward rather than crafty in his dealings; none the less contemporary experience shows that princes who have achieved great things have been those who have given their word lightly, who have known how to trick men with their cunning, and who, in the end, have overcome those abiding by honest principles.

(Machiavelli, 1961: 54)

Machiavelli does not exactly condone mendacity in the passage above; he merely argues that it is unavoidable. Elyot and Machiavelli might appear to be polar opposites, but while they differ on the question of deceit, there are also a number of areas where the two writers agree. Machiavelli reaches typically humanist prescriptions on the question of flattery, and like many other authors he stresses the importance of choosing counsellors wisely (1961: 73–5).

Nevertheless, Machiavelli's rejection of standard moral precepts seems to have made *The Prince* unacceptable in many quarters. Machiavelli was widely demonised, not least by Shakespeare's own reference to 'the murderous Machiavel' (*3 Henry VI* 3.2.193). However, he was not the only thinker to reject the Erasmian ideal of virtue inculcated by education – a topic ignored in *The Prince*. In Italy, Guicciardini and Botero advanced more cautious arguments for favouring political expedience over virtuous conduct in specific circumstances (Skinner, 1978: 248). In England, Stephen Gardiner produced a treatise between 1563 and 1565 which, according to its editor, 'follows Machiavelli closely in essentials' and directly quotes large sections of *The Prince* (Gardiner, 1975: 18, 16). This text shows that Machiavellian principles were being applied to the analysis of British history well before Shakespeare's time: Gardiner compares the cruelty of William I to the mercy of Henry VI, judging in William's favour on the basis of results (Gardiner, 1975: 111r–111v).

It has frequently been observed that politics, as it is represented in many of the history plays and particularly in the two parts of *Henry IV*, is always 'Machiavellian' (see, for example, Bevington, 1968: 245; Leggatt, 1988: 90; Rackin, 1990: 80). But it is unclear whether this would have been perceived as a dangerous idea in early modern England. The idea that politics inevitably functioned in this way may well have been more widespread than the condemnation of Machiavelli might lead one to believe. Similar expressions of cynicism about the court, as mentioned above in relation to Wyatt, date back at least to the 1530s. The plays, despite the apparently cynical view of politics that they present, do insist on a difference between good and bad princes, while acknowledging that all princes are required to be deceitful.

William Hazlitt, the first Shakespeare critic to regard Henry's character in an unfavourable light, observed disapprovingly that 'in all these plays ... the moral inference does not at all depend upon the nature of the actions, but on the dignity or meanness of the persons committing them' (1906: 288). This suggestion is interesting because early modern writers on kingship tend to distinguish between a good prince and an evil prince on the basis of internal moral character, rather than observable behaviour or stated policies (Bushnell, 1990: 38). Erasmus, for example, writes:

> A beneficent prince ... is a living likeness of God, who is at once good and powerful. His goodness makes him want to help all; his power makes him able to do so. On the other hand, an evil prince, who is like a plague to his country, is the incarnation of the devil, who has great power joined with his wickedness.
>
> (Erasmus, 1936: 157)

This seems very clear and unambiguous, but it is a little short on detail. While Erasmus stresses the importance of clemency and forgiveness (209), and argues that the model for any prince should be Jesus Christ (177), this does not seem to imply that a prince must always act leniently. In another passage, Erasmus argues that flatterers should 'suffer punishment (even death, if the crime should call for it) as an example to others. This should not seem cruel to anyone, since we inflict the death penalty ... on a thief who has chanced to steal a few dollars' (194). Erasmus does go on to make some practical suggestions on such subjects as fiscal policy and treaties, but these ideas are presented after the distinction between a Christian prince and an evil tyrant has been established on moral – and subjective – grounds. The practical advice is offered to a reader who is already assumed to be a good prince.

Another way of distinguishing between tyrants and just rulers was the Aristotelian idea that a tyrant rules for himself, while a just ruler rules for the benefit of the state (Bushnell, 1990: 48). *Henry V* makes use of this principle. Henry claims to the French ambassadors that he rules for the benefit of country and people – 'We are no tyrant but a Christian king' – and he reinforces this point in condemning the traitors Scroop, Grey and Cambridge to death:

> Touching our person seek we no revenge,
> But we our kingdom's safety must so tender,
> Whose ruin you have sought, that to her laws
> We do deliver you.
>
> (2.2.175–8)

Henry's pardon of the man who 'railed upon our person' but posed no threat to the state contrasts with his severity towards the real traitors. Henry's thoughts in the passage above represent exactly what a good king ought to feel, according to most sixteenth-century writers on kingship. Bodin, for example, argues that the good king 'seuerely reuengeth the publique iniuries done against the state, and easily pardoneth the wrongs done vnto himselfe', while the tyrant 'most cruelly reuengeth his owne, and pardoneth that which is done against others' (1606: 212). While Bodin presents this as a distinction between good kings and bad kings, it is taken for granted that *any* king will pardon some crimes and punish others. Similarly, Erasmus considers it entirely possible for tyrants to do things which are beneficial for their people; it is just that they do this 'only in so far as it redounds to their personal advantage' (1936: 161). Even an apparently beneficial act must be judged by the intentions behind it, and not by its outcome.

The difficulty with Bodin's view, and with Henry's assertion quoted above, is a problem for any answer based on the internal, subjective states of the ruler.

Henry's actual act – the execution of the traitors – is one with an uncertain moral status. Done for the good of the state it is praiseworthy; but exactly the same decision, made in a spirit of vengeance, would fit a widely accepted definition of tyranny. The reasoning behind the ruler's decision is necessarily concealed, and the acts of the ruler are also subject to rhetorical description, by courtiers and historians – or even playwrights. This means that a cruel act can be rhetorically transformed by *paradiastole* into a just one, or a merciful act into a weak or partial one. Henry claims that the execution of the traitors is just because he is only thinking of the security of the kingdom, but the audience only has his word for it.

The only occasion in *Henry V* on which the king speaks to the audience – in contrast to Richard, who repeatedly soliloquises in order to proclaim his own villainy – is in his speech on ceremony. The fact that this is Henry's only soliloquy signals that he is telling the audience what he really thinks; virtually everything Henry says in public is rhetoric aimed at producing a result. As a result, the speech is arguably Henry's only introspective act, and it is in part a forlorn protest about the heavy burden of kingship:

> What infinite heart's-ease
> Must kings neglect, that private men enjoy!
> And what have kings, that privates have not too,
> Save ceremony, save general ceremony?
>
> (4.1.233–6)

This speech goes on in this vein for about 50 lines, understandably striking Annabel Patterson as 'excruciating in its self-regard' (1989: 77). However, what Henry reveals about his innermost self is in line with humanist prescriptions as to the inner states of a good prince. A similar description of the cares of the king can be found in *The Education of a Christian Prince* (Erasmus, 1936: 162), in which the king's discomfort with his position is described as a precondition for his fitness to rule (160). Of all Shakespeare's kings in the two tetralogies of history plays from *Richard II* to *Henry VI*, the only one who does not at some point express dissatisfaction with his position is *Richard III*. His thoughts about kingship, expressed in *3 Henry VI*, are very different: 'How sweet a thing it is to wear a crown/Within whose circuit is Elysium' (1.2.28–9).[3] To anyone familiar with the humanist teachings, this view would disqualify Richard as a suitable king. By contrast, Henry's only soliloquy seeks to demonstrate that, according to standards that were widely accepted at the time, he is a good king. All of his deceptions and evasions, however disquieting they may seem, are simply an inevitable part of politics. In Shakespeare's plays, mendacity is part of a king's job.

Even if Henry's mendacious behaviour is justified, however, it might appear troubling that the play which represents him seems, via the chorus, to mislead the audience. It has frequently been pointed out that the choric interpretation of events in *Henry V* is often at odds with what is presented on stage (Danson, 1983: 29; Patterson, 1989: 77). As the choric speeches constitute a rhetorical (and apparently misleading) description of the action in *Henry V*, this discrepancy adds a further complication to the interpretation of ethical stance in the play.

A similar problem is present in *Richard III*, as described earlier; Margaret's speech to Elizabeth implies that rhetorical techniques could potentially be used to exaggerate Richard's villainy. This possibility is one of which educated audience members in early modern England would have been well aware, given the prominence of rhetoric in early modern educational curricula, and mentioning it in a play would seem to draw attention to the play's own rhetorical distortion of Richard's character, especially since poetry, drama and rhetoric were regarded as almost synonymous in early modern culture (Rebhorn, 1995: 18). That both plays draw attention to their own acts of rhetorical distortion seems disquieting. Nevertheless, there is no evidence that either of the plays was perceived as problematic in its own time, and this seems to require explanation.

Unease with rhetoric was not unknown in early modern Europe. The principle that an argument can always be advanced on either side of a question – *in utramque partem* – raised serious concerns about the morality of rhetoricians: one critic of rhetoric, Heinrich Agrippa, gives the example of classical orators who could with equal ease 'perswade righteous and unrightuous causes' (1575: 19). Other theorists of rhetoric often recognised this possibility without passing moral judgement; one such writer, Thomas Wilson, refers matter-of-factly to occasions when 'we speake against our owne conscience in an euill matter' (1580: 8). Quite apart from being open to abuse, rhetoric was, according to its critics, inherently dishonest. Wilson's discussion of amplification, discussed above, is a case in point, and even the upright Erasmus is happy to advocate the use of 'terms of exaggeration' such as 'when we call a cruel man, a torturer' (1963: 35). 'Amplification' could easily be regarded as lying, and this point was not lost on Agrippa, who bluntly refers to rhetoric as exactly that (1575: 17).

In spite of these concerns, however, critics of rhetoric were in a small minority in the sixteenth century. Rhetoric was an essential part of the early modern educational curriculum, and its perceived importance as a political skill was also great. George Puttenham's *Arte of English Poesie* claims that poets (and therefore rhetoricians) were 'the first Legislators and polititians in the world' (1869: 22), and goes on to describe poetry as a precondition for politics. Puttenham claims that humans would have continued to live 'like the wild beasts' without eloquence, because no one would have been able to persuade them to live in an ordered society. This claim, dating back to Cicero, was a common one in the early modern discourse of rhetoric. Such a powerful tool could not be ignored; it ought to be used as a force for good.

Ensuring that the prince was virtuous, in line with humanist recommendations, was a task in which rhetoric could play an important role. When discussing how a future prince should be taught the difference between a good and a bad ruler, Erasmus suggests that the following 'pictures' should be drawn in order to encourage goodness in the child. A good prince is to be described as 'a sort of celestial creature, more like to a divine being than a mortal, complete in all the virtues; born for the common good; yea, sent by the God above to help the affairs of mortals' (1936: 162). An evil prince, meanwhile, is a frightful, loathsome beast, formed of a dragon, wolf, lion, viper, bear, and like creatures; with six hundred eyes all over it, teeth everywhere, fearful from all angles, and with hooked claws; with never satiated hunger, fattened on human vitals, and reeking with human blood.

(Erasmus, 1936: 163)

The excessive nature of these pictures is a particularly obvious example of rhetorical amplification. Erasmus advocates drastically exaggerating the vice of the tyrant and the virtue of the good prince. The purpose of this exaggeration is to educate a prince who will be genuinely good – although presumably not quite a 'celestial creature', as Erasmus must have realised.

This kind of rhetorical amplification is applied to the characters of Henry and Richard in Shakespeare's plays. Rather than being used in order to educate a prince, the plays are designed, in part, to educate the populace. The over-the-top pictures they present make the officially sanctioned version of recent English history clearer; as Erasmus puts it, rhetorical hyperbole is a 'lie' by which 'we come to truth' (1963: 35). The fact that the plays also draw attention to their own rhetorical distortions need not be understood as undermining the representation of the two kings, since this particular kind of distortion was so widely celebrated at the time – not least for its didactic value.

What is interesting is that such distortion was necessary at all. Many sixteenth-century political theorists struggled with the problem that tyranny and justice can be difficult to distinguish by outward appearances. In the two plays discussed here, it is easy to identify Richard as an evil character because of his long soliloquies and asides, and Henry's heroism has only relatively recently begun to be questioned. But even in *Henry V* and *Richard III*, plays that were long accepted as archetypal portraits of a great king and an evil tyrant, a significant degree of similarity between the two protagonists can be detected. The parallels between these two characters indicate the urgency of the problem posed by Bodin, which was quoted at the start of this article: how can anybody tell a tyrant apart from a just ruler, without soliloquies to help them? The authorities' awareness that this was a difficult matter, and their concern that it should not be attempted at all by the common people, was communicated directly to the populace through the *Homilie Agaynst Disobedience and Wylful Rebellion* (1570):

those princes whom some subjectes do thinke to be verye godlye, and under whose gouernment they reioyce to lyve: some other subjectes do take the same to be evyll and ungodly, and do wishe for a chaunge. If therefore all subiectes that mislike of their prince, shoulde rebell, no Realme shoulde ever be without rebellion.

(B1v–B2)

This passage makes clear that there will always be disagreement about the virtues of any ruler in any country, which is why the problem raised by Bodin was of such great concern. Whether the king appears to be a tyrant or a just ruler is dependent on one's perspective. Even in comparing the best of kings with the worst of kings, we are still looking at two kings – and, therefore, two liars. Outside the theatre (and even inside it) the similarities between them may be as significant as the differences. This idea, which might strike a modern critic as subversive of the early modern political order at first glance, is tacitly acknowledged in writings that were entirely acceptable to the dominant orthodoxy of the time. The plays likewise suggest a great degree of similarity between Richard and Henry, even as they stress the differences between them.

Disclosure statement

No potential conflict of interest was reported by the author.

Notes

1. As Stephen Greenblatt points out, he is also 'virtually the only Shakespearean ruler with a high-minded, ethical goal' (2009: 68).
2. Norfolk seems to have a high opinion of Richard's strategic brain, praising his battle plan and calling him 'warlike sovereign' (5.3.302). Richard is also successful in war in the *Henry VI* plays.
3. Richard, too, is wise enough to conceal his true feelings about the throne, asking '[w]ill you enforce me to a world of cares?' when offered it by the Lord Mayor (*Richard III* 3.7.222).

References

Agrippa von Nettesheim, Heinrich (1575). *The Vanity of Arts and Sciences*. Trans. J. Sandford. Early English Books Online. 29 January 2014. http://eebo.chadwyck.com.ludwig.lub.lu.se/home.

An Homilie Agaynst Disobedience and Wylful Rebellion (1570). Early English Books Online. 29 January 2014. http://eebo.chadwyck.com.ludwig.lub.lu.se/home.

Bevington, David (1968). *Tudor Drama and Politics*. Cambridge, MA: Harvard UP.

Bodin, Jean (1606). *The Six Bookes of a Common-Weale*. Trans. R. Knolles. Early English Books Online. 29 January 2014. <http://eebo.chadwyck.com.ludwig.lub.lu.se/home>.

Bushnell, Rebecca (1990). *Tragedies of Tyrants*. Ithaca: Cornell UP.

Danson, Lawrence (1983). 'Henry V: King, Chorus, and Critics.' *Shakespeare Quarterly* 34.1: 27–43.

Elyot, Thomas (1531). *The Boke Named the Gouernour*. Early English Books Online. 29 January 2014. <http://eebo.chadwyck.com.ludwig.lub.lu.se/home>.

Erasmus, Desiderius (1936). *The Education of a Christian Prince*. Trans. L.K. Born. New York: Columbia UP.

Erasmus, Desiderius (1963). *On Copia of Words and Ideas*. Trans. D. King and D. Rix. Milwaukee, WI: Marquette UP.

Fitter, Chris (2002). 'A Tale of Two Branaghs: Henry V, Ideology and the Mekong Agincourt.' *Shakespeare's History Plays*. Ed. R.J.C. Watt. London: Pearson. 169–83.

Gardiner, Stephen (1975). *A Machiavellian Treatise*. Ed. and Trans. P. Donaldson. Cambridge: Cambridge UP.

Greenblatt, Stephen (2009). 'Shakespeare and the Ethics of Authority.' *Shakespeare and Early Modern Political Thought*. Eds David Armitage, Conal Condren and Andrew Fitzmaurice. Cambridge: Cambridge UP. 64–79.

Hazlitt, William (1906). *Characters of Shakespear's Plays*. London: J M Dent.

Leggatt, Alexander (1988). *Shakespeare's Political Drama*. London: Routledge.

Machiavelli, Nicolo (1961). *The Prince*. Trans. George Bull. London: Penguin.

Patterson, Annabel (1989). *Shakespeare and the Popular Voice*. Oxford: Blackwell.

Puttenham, George (1869). *The Arte of English Poesie*. Ed. Edward Arber. London: Edward Arber.

Rackin, Phyllis (1990). *Stages of History: Shakespeare's English Chronicles*. London: Routledge.

Rebhorn, Wayne (1995). *The Emperor of Men's Minds*. Ithaca: Cornell UP.

Ribner, Irving (1957). *The English History Play in the Age of Shakespeare*. Princeton: Princeton UP.

Shakespeare, William (1981). *King Henry IV, Part 2*. Ed. A. Humphreys. London: A&C Black.

Shakespeare, William (1995). *King Henry V*. Ed. T. Craik. London: Routledge.

Shakespeare, William (2001). *King Henry VI, Part 3*. Eds J. Cox and E. Rasmussen. London: A&C Black.

Shakespeare, William (2002). *King Henry IV, Part 1*. Ed. David Scott Kastan. London: A&C Black.

Shakespeare, William (2009). *King Richard III*. Ed. James Siemon. London: A&C Black.

Sharpe, Kevin (2009). *Selling the Tudor Monarchy*. New Haven, CT: Yale UP.

Siemon, James (2009). Introduction. *King Richard III*. London: A&C Black.

Skinner, Quentin (1978). *The Foundations of Modern Political Thought*. Vol. 1. 2 vols. Cambridge: Cambridge UP.

Skinner, Quentin (2002). *Visions of Politics*. Vol. 2. 3 vols. Cambridge: Cambridge UP.

Tillyard, Eustace (1944). *Shakespeare's History Plays*. Harmondsworth: Penguin.

Wilson, Thomas (1580). *The Arte of Rhetoricke*. Early English Books Online. 29 January 2014. <http://eebo.chadwyck.com.ludwig.lub.lu.se/home>.

Eric Pudney studied Philosophy and Politics at the University of Warwick and Literature at Lund University in Sweden, and is now a doctoral candidate in English Literature at Lund. His doctoral thesis deals with the representation of witchcraft in sixteenth- and seventeenth-century drama. He has published articles on Oscar Wilde's *The Picture of Dorian Gray* and Cormac McCarthy's *The Road*.

Shanyn Altman

'AN ANXIOUS ENTANGLING AND PERPLEXING OF CONSCIENCES': JOHN DONNE AND CATHOLIC RECUSANT MENDACITY

This article argues that, in Donne's view, the taking of an oath should benefit society rather than reflect the true interiority of the subject, and that a crucial aspect of his defence of the Jacobean Oath of Allegiance in Pseudo-Martyr *is the representation of mendacity as a Christian virtue. It further contends that critics who portray Donne's support of the State as being at odds with his religious beliefs have misread the argument in* Pseudo-Martyr, *which indicates that the safest way to achieve salvation is not through the Church but through the State.*

Duplicity and disguise were central aspects in the everyday experience of Catholics living in post-Reformation England. Having been born into a family that had suffered greatly for obeying the Roman doctrine, John Donne was all too aware of this reality and the theme of deception came to pervade his works.[1] In his polemical tract *Pseudo-Martyr*, mendacity is presented as a crucial survival tactic for Catholics who feared that their religious conscience was being compromised. Written in 1609 and published the following year, this text offers a defence of the Oath of Allegiance, which was enforced by James VI and I in 1606 as a response to the Gunpowder Plot, and which controversially required Catholics to acknowledge the authority of the king over that of the pope. The main premise of Donne's argument is that, although every individual has an inherent duty to be loyal to the State, this loyalty does not necessitate an indefinite and logically consequent binding of the conscience. 'If your owne just and due preservation, worke nothing upon you,' Donne writes with reference to a subject's duty to occasionally disguise his true intentions, 'yet have some pitie and compassion towards your Countrey' (1993: 26). The emphasis here is on how the taking of an oath benefits the State rather than the individual. Such a view challenged the popular notion in early modern England that an 'oath was the measure of the conscience' and hence a true reflection on the interiority of the subject (Spurr, 2004: 159).[2] For Donne, an oath acted as a mode of uniformity to prevent the conscience from being measured.

Pseudo-Martyr's defence of the State has often led critics such as David Norbrook (1990: 16) and Kate Gartner Frost (1990: 40) to regard the text negatively as a 'quest for advancement' and an attempt 'to gain royal favor'. Such a view implies that Donne's endorsement of the Oath was a morally compromising act of obedience to the king that used mendacity for personal gain. If this argument is accepted, scholars could be forgiven for agreeing with John Carey's (1981: 33) curious assertion that when Donne produced *Pseudo-Martyr* 'he was using, at best, only half his mind'. The purpose of this article is to establish that far from being a 'journalistic work' that simply reflects contemporary attitudes regarding the Oath of Allegiance (Raspa, 1993: xiii), *Pseudo-Martyr* is a part of the political dialogue that was shaping these attitudes through its suggestion that mendacity can, under certain circumstances, be considered a Christian virtue. It will argue that to discredit Donne for supporting the king is not only to underestimate the complexity of *Pseudo-Martyr* but also to misread the text's distinction between honesty and political virtue. Martin Jay (2010: 102) rightly notes that certain Renaissance cultures developed 'a secularized version of the religious practice of sacrifice for the solidarity of the community', whereby the 'moral rectitude of the private man would be sacrificed for a "higher good"', and that this formed the basis of eighteenth-century polite society. As a forward-thinking text that endorses what the Renaissance author Baldesar Castiglione (1959: 43) would have termed 'honest dissimulation', *Pseudo-Martyr* reflects on this notion of society.[3]

The primary aim of *Pseudo-Martyr* was to exonerate the conscience of the individual who interpreted the following words from the Oath as heresy:

> I do from my heart abhor, detest and abjure as impious and heretical this damnable doctrine and position that princes which be excommunicated and deprived by the pope may be deposed or murdered by their subjects or any whatsoever. And I do believe and in my conscience am resolved, that neither the pope nor any person whatsoever hath power to absolve me of this oath [...]. And all these things I do plainly and sincerely acknowledge and swear, according to these express words by me spoken, and according to the plain and common sense and understanding of the same words without any equivocation or mental evasion or secret reservation whatsoever.
>
> (Kenyon, 1986: 170–1)

Despite James's claims in *An Apologie for the Oath of Allegiance* that his intention was 'not to intrap nor inthrall [the Catholics'] consciences', and that taking the Oath was solely a case of civil obedience to separate radicals from loyalists (1609: 22), the wording of the Oath suggests otherwise. In associating the pope with such terms as 'impious', 'heretical' and 'damnable', the phrasing and tone of the Oath, as well as the sweeping dismissal of the pope's authority both to overthrow an excommunicated king and to give absolution, was considered by many Catholics to be partisan and controversial. As Michael Questier (1997: 311–13) argues, the Oath was a 'diabolically effective polemical cocktail' which 'should be understood as an exceptionally subtle and well-constructed rhetorical essay in the exercise of state power', and 'possibly the most lethal measure against Romish dissent ever to reach the statute book'.[4] Recognising the danger inherent in an Oath that was designed to prevent forms of mendacity such as 'equivocation', 'mental evasion' and 'secret reservation', Pope Paul V banned the taking of the Oath in 1606 and again in 1607, which meant that Catholics were forced to declare publicly whether their loyalty lay with the Church or with the State. If it lay with the former, the fear was execution for treason. If it lay with the latter, the fear was eternal damnation.

The contentious nature of the Oath generated a pamphlet war across Europe concerning the authority of the king and the pope. In this literary war, arguments and counter-arguments were articulated through the use of casuistry, a popular mode by which cases of conscience had been explored for three centuries and which had become, during Donne's lifetime, 'increasingly confined to works of "practical" instruction' (Malloch, 1962: 58). The purpose of such casuistry, explains Olga Valbuena (2000: 69), was to provide 'a mode of rational deliberation that negotiated conflicting obligations between spiritual and temporal allegiance or between two incompatible laws'. While Roman casuists placed an emphasis on allowing the conscience to be guided by external authorities, Anglican casuists encouraged an acquisition of knowledge that would turn 'the perplexed subject back onto his own conscience' (70). By demonstrating how language can be wielded for different purposes, Donne distinguishes the two schools of casuistry as good and bad. The 'Romane Authors' are presented in *Pseudo-Martyr* as self-serving and malicious, since they 'build Equivocation, which is like a Tower of *Babel*' in order to 'get above all earthly Magistracie' (Donne, 1993: 57). Roman casuistry, for Donne, is intrinsically deceptive because it manipulates already existing arguments to justify a standpoint; it is an end within itself. Anglican casuistry, in contrast, sacrifices short-term truth for the sake of long-term truth; it is a means by which a person can justify his or her actions without compromising his or her spiritual development. Adopting Aquinas's definition of 'conscience' as *'an Act by which we apply our knowledge [of good and evil] to some particular thing'* (Donne, 1993: 173),[5] Donne argues that the conscience develops in relation to a person's understanding of religion. In this sense, casuistry ought to inform but not seek to capture the conscience. With the theme of deception at the heart of Donne's evaluation of Catholic casuistry in particular, the text illustrates how mendacity can be viewed as either sinful, if used for selfish ends, or virtuous, if used as a tool in the search for religious truth.

Texts like *Pseudo-Martyr* became necessary in the years following 1606 because, although many Catholics were unhesitant about swearing their allegiance to the king, there remained a resistance to the terms of the Oath. This is demonstrated by historical evidence showing that many Catholics attempted to compose different versions of the Oath which 'omitted the offending aspects of it' (Questier, 2008: 22). It is crucial to note, however, that the majority of these modified versions were rejected by the State and that, in some instances, the individual making the proposition was executed (22–6). The severity of the State's reaction suggests that the question of what it meant to be loyal to the Crown extended further than simply complying with the law. What was being demanded of subjects was an abstraction such as 'fidelytie',[6] which demonstrates the State's desire to control the uncontrollable in an attempt to eradicate all mendacity. On this point, Questier (1997: 329) concludes that although religious opinions 'eventually became a matter of private conscience in which the state did not interfere … the process did not commence with the Jacobean oath of allegiance'. The process did commence, however, with certain responses to the Oath that encouraged a separation of political responsibilities and the private conscience. *Pseudo-Martyr* is a particularly revealing example of this emerging tradition. As a text which presents a person's 'owne preservation' as a 'natural duety' (Donne, 1993: 155), Donne's tract argues that grand gestures such as dying for a refusal of the Oath are more likely to imperil one's soul than pave the way to salvation.

The need for political mendacity in matters concerning the Oath arose out of two key issues. Firstly, in the phrase 'I do believe and in my conscience am resolved', the Oath evidently stipulated a resolution of conscience, which led to the belief among some Catholic clergy that 'full conformity was the natural corollary of accepting the oath' (Questier, 1997: 326). Robert Persons (1608: 9), for example, inquires: 'Why are Recusants punished, & fyned for Recusancy, though they take the *Oath* of *Allegiance*? Is not Recusancie a cause of Conscience?' Secondly, James I's popularisation of divine right, as well as his public identification with King Solomon, who represented both State and religion, complicated the claim that the Oath would not interfere with matters of the Church.[7] Donne dismisses this contradiction by distinguishing between 'Articles of faith & jurisdiction' to eliminate the supposed conflict between the king and the pope. The two governing bodies are able to coexist, he writes, because they are dependent upon one another: the political authority 'by his laws keeps us in the way of heaven', while the spiritual authority ensures 'that we live virtuously and innocently in this life for society here' (Donne, 1993: 39).

Throughout the text, both the State and the Church are presented as paths leading to God. Donne argues, however, that since religion is susceptible to human error and 'mis-interpretations' (1993: 13), it is safer to bind one's conscience to the king. *Pseudo-Martyr* emphasises that the primary function of the State is to 'conserve' society 'in *Peace* and *Religion*' (131); should an individual threaten the State by not adhering to the law, it follows, then, that such an individual would also threaten the stability of religion. This idea is clarified in *Biathanatos*, a work that Donne was writing around the same time as *Pseudo-Martyr*, which contends that God comes 'nearer to us, first by the Law and then by Grace' because the law 'is given us a light, that we might not stumble' (Donne, 1984: 109 and 120). Yet, although the State provides the safer route to God, Donne makes it clear that no earthly authority is absolute: he only writes to remind readers that 'your Obedience here, may prepare your admission into the heavenly *Hierusalem*' (1993: 28). Unlike James, who defends the view that monarchs are directly appointed by God, Donne argues that the natural inclination of 'all wise men' in society leads them to 'chuse' one who is 'aptest to worke their end', and it is only then that 'God instils such a power as we wish to be in that person' (131–2). The implication of this is that governments are established by and for the sole benefit of the commonwealth. Since the stability of the government and, by extension, the prosperity of religion, relies on the unity of individuals within society, Donne presents the need for mendacity in matters of conformity as a way to preserve rather than to deceive the State.

This idea is explicated in *Biathanatos*, which argues that although self-homicide may be permissible under certain circumstances, it is extremely sinful to die for treason (Donne, 1984: 109). In defending the Oath as a 'lawfull acte' which protects rather than persecutes the subject, *Pseudo-Martyr* suggests that the conflicted Catholic 'destroyes himselfe' and 'abuse[s] Gods mercie by not using it' (1993: 155). The image of the Jacobean conformist, however, would have seemed at odds with the popular – albeit unofficial – notion of a martyr. Coming at the end of a tradition of martyrologies and counter-martyrologies, which John Foxe had established in London in 1563 with the first publication of the *Actes and Monuments*, the martyr was often presented as a figure prepared to seal his doctrine with blood in the face of persecution. In noting that death and martyrdom were often viewed as being inextricably connected at the time, John R. Knott states that: 'Despite the prominence of examinations in Foxe's narrative, and their importance in defining the faith of prospective martyrs, it is the death scenes that stick in the mind' (2010: 78). Such literary representations of grisly but heroic deaths did not reflect the law of the time, which saw '[s]uicides being tried posthumously' for committing a 'heinous crime' at the 'instigation of the devil' (MacDonald, 1989: 69). This law echoed traditional views on suicide presented by significant figures such as Augustine and Aquinas, which condemned the act of self-murder as a homicide against an innocent person.

'The great relevance of John Donne's *Pseudo-Martyr*,' writes Anthony Raspa (1993: xvii):

was that it addressed itself to minority English Catholics for whom lay waiting the uncivilized horror of execution by being hanged, drawn and quartered, and dissolved in boiling oil at the traitor's gibbet at Tyburn outside London, with the possible inclusion in the Catholic calendar of martyrs as their reward.

If Donne was going to influence political decisions, he would need to redefine the figure of the martyr. For this purpose, he presents true martyrdom 'in the proper and restrain'd sense and acceptation, that is, of *Consummate Martyrdome*', as proceeding from disguise and the use of discretion. Should a person be executed as a result of provoking his persecutor by being too zealous about his faith, that person would not be considered a martyr but rather a '*Biothanatum*, a selfe-murderer', and therefore a pseudo-martyr. This view challenges ideas generated by the English Jesuits Edmund Campion and Robert Persons, who, in 1580, insisted upon 'uncompromising recusancy' (Lake and Questier, 2011: 49). In his *A Brief Discours Contayning Certayne Reasons why Catholiques Refuse to goe to Church*, Persons argues that a 'Catholicke in minde, may not goe to the Churches or service of the contrarie religion' because, should that doctrine be 'false doctrine, and consequently venemous unto the hearer, I may not venture my soul to be infected with the same' (1580: 6). *Pseudo-Martyr* argues, however, that the purpose of conformity and disguise is not merely to stay alive. It is to preserve the body physically so that the conscience may suffer in the proper Christian fashion. Donne's view on the matter is expressed most succinctly in his poem 'A Litanie': 'O, to some | Not to be martyrs, is a martyrdom' (ll. 89–90).

Thus, in both *Pseudo-Martyr* and *Biathanatos*, Donne aims to widen the gap between true and false martyrdom. The former is presented as being concerned with the glorification of God, and the latter is characterised as an epidemic of suicide. As Andrew Hadfield (forthcoming) rightly notes, there is an indication in *Biathanatos* that the 'Catholic Church celebrates its martyrs without question even though the historical record does not support or justify what they believe'; for this reason, many may well be considered 'pseudo-martyrs held up as examples to encourage yet more pseudo-martyrs, very close to, if not actually, a case of mass suicide'. Those refusing the Oath in the hope of achieving martyrdom are thus condemned in *Pseudo-Martyr* for 'hunting and pursuing' their own death, '[f]irst, over the tops of mountains', which is 'the Popes *Spirituall power*' and then 'through thicke and entangling woods, without ways in or out, that is his *Temporall power*', and not to mention the 'darke caves and dens of his Chamber Epistles, his *Breves*' (1993: 161). With the '*Breves*' here referring to the pope's banning of the Oath in 1606 and 1607, this image portrays the dangerously deliberate (or deliberately dangerous) 'pretences to Martyrdome' involved in refusing the Oath out of 'blinde and stupid obedience'. In order to counter this type of '*ambition and greediness of vaine glorie*' which does not result in the glorification of God, Donne reinforces the idea that the protection of one's life is of prime importance because 'we must understand that our body is not our owne' (Donne, 1984: 23). If one were to deliberately put himself in danger, it is argued, he would despoil himself or herself 'of the benefite of Martyrdome' (1993: 160). This argument follows Augustine's line of reasoning in *City of God* that 'it is plainly unlawful for any one' to die on purpose due to the belief that they have been 'promised a mansion of eternity at their deaths' (1610: I. 22).[8]

Donne suggests that instead of embarking on a dangerous quest for martyrdom that may result in death, the conflicted Catholic should strive to achieve a *living* martyrdom; that is, a martyrdom attained through the endurance of suffering in life. The preface to *Biathanatos* states that:

> Contemplative, and bookish men must of necessity be more quarrellsome then others, because they contend not about matter of fact, nor can determine theyr controversies by any certayne witnesses, nor judges. But as long as they go towards Peace, that is Truith, it is no matter which way.

(Donne, 1984: 31)

The point here is that any constructive and well-informed argument that is driven by a desire to discover religious truth can be considered valid; for such 'bookish men', therefore, there are no right or wrong arguments, only good or bad. This idea is portrayed in 'Satyre III' (Donne, 2010: 394–5), in which 'Truth stands' on a 'Craggèd and steep' hill, difficult to reach but necessary to seek out. Despite the 'body's pains' in attaining such 'hard knowledge', each individual must work to find and 'Keep the truth' that he or she has discovered. 'To stand inquiring right,' the speaker asserts, 'is not to stray.' Similarly, in *Pseudo-Martyr* the reader is reminded to imitate '*Justinians* great Officer *Tiberius*', who, 'out of reverence to the signe of the Crosse [...] removed a Marble stone from the Pavement' and then another and another until he found 'a great plenty of treasure' without having had this treasure 'in his hope, nor purpose, nor desire beforehand'.[9] This story, which portrays an image of living martyrdom, indicates that the 'treasure and crowne of

Martyrdome' cannot be sought, but only discovered incidentally as a reward for hard work and suffering in the proper manner (Donne, 1993: 32). *Pseudo-Martyr* thus suggests that the Catholic who binds his conscience to the king, sacrificing short-term truth for the sake of long-term truth in order to serve the State, may achieve a living martyrdom.

The advocacy of mendacity which necessitates, in Donne's view, a condemnation of Catholic casuistry and an elaboration of the concept of living martyrdom, has important connections to Anglican casuistry. This is apparent in *Pseudo-Martyr*'s emphasis on the formation of the conscience, as well as in the style and structure of the work. Despite Donne's indisputable knowledge of and interest in the genre, research regarding his representation of casuistry is surprisingly limited. Yet, those who have acknowledged casuistry as a crucial aspect in works such as *Pseudo-Martyr*, *Biathanatos*, *Ignatius His Conclave* and 'Satyre III' have, remarkably, tended to portray Donne's attitude towards the genre as 'contradictory' and 'ambivalent' (Slights, 1972: 88). In her article '"To Stand Inquiring Right": The Casuistry of Donne's "Satyre III"', Camille Wells Slights argues, for instance, that Donne was simultaneously 'fascinated' and 'repelled' by Catholic casuistry (87), and, in her later book *The Casuistical Tradition* (1992), proceeds to present Donne as a failed casuist whose 'casuistry lacks the scope and general applicability of comprehensive discussions or principles' because 'his argument relies too heavily on the methods he condemns' (1992: 141–9). Similarly, Olga Valbuena states that although Donne 'appears to denounce and certainly does satirize the methods and especially the motives of Jesuit casuists and equivocators', he finally comes to depend 'on their methods to defend the liberty of the individual faced with a practical moral impasse with moral consequences' (2000: 66). Although both critical accounts are valuable in assessing Donne's attack on the Roman casuist by teasing out the differences between Catholic and Anglican casuistry, neither recognise the irony that underlines Donne's mockery of the genre. He is not repelled by the *use* of casuistry, but by its *misuse*. By creating a dynamic in which the casuist's polemical discourse is its own destruction, *Pseudo-Martyr* demonstrates a clearly comprehensive scope and understanding of the general principles of casuistry. Through a satirical application of these principles, Donne undermines the validity of oversubtle arguments which abuse their inclination towards mendacity, in order to direct readers back to their own consciences.

An example of this occurs in chapter VIII, when Donne comments that 'we may at once lay open the infirmity, and insufficiency of [the Roman casuists'] *Rules*, and apply the same to our present purpose' (1993: 167). In the context of a chapter which is essentially a playful exercise in the art of argument, this comment demonstrates that Donne uses the methods of the Roman casuist deliberately in order to exploit the dangerous consequences of sophistry. These 'Rules give no infallible direction to the conscience', he writes, and cannot therefore be used as a basis for making important moral decisions. Donne's point is made explicit when he applies the Roman casuists' methods to his own argument to demonstrate the faulty logic by which Catholics risk being misled – a section of *Pseudo-Martyr* which Slights describes as being 'too complicated to treat adequately' (1992: 148). Yet it is precisely the complicated nature of Donne's argument that serves to mock the Roman casuist, since he intentionally makes his point in an obscure fashion to parody what he considers to be the obscure style of casuistical reasoning. In discussing the principle of '*Metum iustum* [justified fear], which is, *such a feare as may fall upon a constant man, and yet not remove his habite of Constancy*', Donne relays the Roman casuists' rule that if a person experiences a justified fear, which includes 'the feare of *Torture, Imprisonment, Exile, Bondage, Losse of temporall goods, or the greater part thereof, or infamy, and dishonour*' as well as of death, then it is acceptable for that person to transgress. The only time that a '*just feare*' may not be applied to a situation is to 'excuse a man from doing any *Evil*, yet that is meant of such an *Evill*, as is *Evill* naturally' (i.e. a deed that is intrinsically evil). Donne applies this line of reasoning to his own argument by stating that the Oath 'is not Naturally Evill' since the authority of a king is '*morall* and *natural*'; the Oath, he goes on to write, only 'became Evill, because it was Forbidden' by the pope. By the logic of the Catholic casuist, then, 'the taking of the Oath were so excusable, as the refusing thereof could not be excused' (1993: 175–6). This *reductio ad absurdum*, to use a term that A.E. Malloch correctly applies to arguments made elsewhere in chapter VIII (1962: 72), exploits the straw man logic of the Catholic casuist who uses a set of general rules to manipulate an argument for his own ends.

Donne's critique of the arguments typical of the Roman casuist in relation to oaths is dramatised in his poem 'Woman's Constancy' (Donne, 2010: 282–3). In this poem, the speaker confronts his lover by anticipating the duplicitous excuses that she could make in order to rescind a 'lovers' contract' (l. 9):

Now thou hast loved me one whole day,
Tomorrow when thou leav'st, what wilt thou say?
Wilt thou then antedate some new-made vow?

(ll. 1–3)

The use of the legal term 'antedate' implies a fraudulent attempt to pervert the course of justice. Since, according to Donne, God comes 'nearer to us, first by the Law and then by Grace' (1984: 109), such an excuse would violate both political and religious virtue. This, along with the ironic use of the phrase 'one whole day' and the idea that such a radical change of mind could occur between 'Now' and 'Tomorrow', highlights the absurdity of this argument which is based on illegality and illogical reasoning.

The next excuse that the speaker anticipates is that the oath was not binding in the first place. Would the lover argue, he asks, that:

We are not just those persons which we were?
Or that oaths made in reverential fear
Of Love and his wrath any may forswear?

(ll. 5–7)

The contents and ironic tone of these lines echo Donne's mockery of '*just feare*' in *Pseudo-Martyr*; a notion on which, as Donne states with reference to the Catholic doctrine of mental reservation, 'the *Casuists* agree' (1993: 175). In both texts, individuals who use fear as an excuse to invalidate an oath after it has been taken are ridiculed. This is because such excuses, or 'scapes' made for the lover's 'own end to justify' (ll. 9–14), are substantiated by the casuistical arguments made by external authorities that disregard truth. The lover, therefore, has 'no way but falsehood to be true' (l. 13). This idea resembles Donne's representation of the Roman casuist in *Pseudo-Martyr*, whose arguments are only true to the falseness of their nature.

In the last four lines of the poem, the speaker quashes the hypothetical arguments which he has previously conjured by appropriating the supposed excuses for his own ends:

> Vain lunatic! Against these scapes I could
> Dispute, and conquer, if I would,
> Which I abstain to do,
> For by tomorrow I may think so too.

(ll. 14–17)

Although 'Woman's Constancy' has often been read as a misogynistic poem,[10] the speaker – though here supposed to be male – is gender-ambiguous. It is relevant that this poem, which at first glance seems to be gender-focused, does not only leave the question of the speaker's sex open, but, in these final lines, renders this question somewhat irrelevant by suggesting that each lover is as fickle as the other. That the speaker could 'Dispute' against these 'scapes' hints at the casuistical convention of responding 'point by point [...] to conclude a debate by leaving no argument unanswered' (North, 2002: 219). The 'conventionality' of such a tactic, explains North, typically 'gave one's opponent a ready-made structure for a counterattack' which perpetuated yet more casuistry, since no argument could be convincing enough to prevent further argument (219). Like chapter VIII of *Pseudo-Martyr*, 'Woman's Constancy' is a playful exercise in the art of argument which parodies the frailty of the human mind that relies on casuistry, instead of the conscience, when making and breaking oaths. On this point, both texts demonstrate how oaths between human beings are susceptible to human error, and so cannot bind the conscience indefinitely. It is therefore vital that a person who swears to an oath only does so with a cautious understanding that as the conscience develops, so such promises may need to be modified.

The idea in *Pseudo-Martyr* that an earthly oath can be broken within the conscience of a subject for a higher cause resonates with Donne's well-known Holy sonnet 'Batter my heart'. In this poem, the speaker begs for the 'three-personed God' to release him of all earthly bonds so that he, the speaker, may embody the Holy Ghost:

> Yet dearly'I love you', and would be lov'd faine,
> But am betroth'd unto your enemy,
> Divorce me, untie, or breake that knot againe [...].

(Donne, 2005: 109)

Although the identity of the 'enemy' is left ambiguous, the motif of marriage and divorce indicates that an oath of some sort has been made to someone or something contrary to God, which recalls the 'lovers' contract' of 'Woman's Constancy'. The speaker's plea for God to 'breake' this 'knot' demonstrates, however, that the breaking of an oath for reasons of virtue would require divine intervention. Unlike the oath made between the speaker and the 'enemy' which, being described in legal terms, relies on outward displays of conformity, the imagined spiritual union between the speaker and God relies on inward desires. At the end of the poem the notion of oath-taking is sexualised as the speaker asks to be 'ravished' by God so that his religious commitment may be consummated. It is only at the point that God has entered into him, making the external internal, that the speaker feels his conscience will be truly bound.

The language of 'Batter my heart', in which the speaker laments that he is 'betroth'd' to God's enemy and craves to be 'enthrall[ed]' by God, as well as the poem's theme of domination, echo the Preface to *Pseudo-Martyr*, in which Donne states that he will not 'betroth or enthral' himself 'to any one science, which should possess or dominate' him (Donne, 1993: 12). Donne's resistance to blind obedience is not limited to the pope, religion or casuistry, but extends to all external authorities including the king. As it is stated in 'Satyre III', monarchs may have the power to 'kill whom they hate' on behalf of God, yet they are merely 'hangmen to fate' (Donne, 2010: 395). This indicates that the monarch does not have jurisdiction over free will and so cannot truly force a subject to follow the State's religion. As such, although 'thou mayest rightly obey power' – and it is important to note that this power is 'rightly' obeyed – a subject must know the 'bounds' of that power and not 'be tied | To man's laws'. To 'choose men's unjust | Power from God claim'd, than God' is classified in this poem as idolatry. This theme is manifested in *Pseudo-Martyr*. Since religious understanding is constantly subject to human error and 'mis-interpretations', the author explains that he has an 'easines, to affoord a sweete and gentle Interpretation, to all professors of Christian Religion, if they shake not the Foundation' (1993: 12–13). By emphasising his 'easines' in accepting different forms of Christianity so long as the 'Foundation', Jesus Christ, is not called into question, Donne here underlines the subtext of *Pseudo-Martyr* that forms his endorsement of political mendacity: the idea that a Catholic who refuses the Oath of Allegiance, either on the grounds that a civil law could bind him spiritually to the king or out of blind obedience to the pope, essentially commits an act of idolatry.

Acknowledgements

I am grateful to Andrew Hadfield, Dennis Flynn, Daniel Starza Smith and Jonathan Buckner for their comments on an earlier draft of this article.

Disclosure statement

No potential conflict of interest was reported by the author.

Notes

1. In the Preface to *Pseudo-Martyr* (1993: 8), Donne outlines the struggle he faced in converting from Catholicism to Protestantism.
2. For a thorough history of the development of the oath throughout history, see Silving (1959).
3. For Castiglione's influence on Donne's ideas about social codes of courtly behaviour, see Peter DeSa Wiggins (2000).
4. For further discussion on the intentions behind the drafting of the Oath and the penalties for refusal, see Questier (2008) and Ryan (1942).
5. Donne is citing Aquinas's *Summa Theologica*, I., Question 79, Article 18, 'conclusion'.
6. Oaths were commonly associated with the term 'fidelytie' during the early modern period. The Oath of Allegiance is referred to as an 'oath of fidelytie' in some key texts that contributed to the allegiance controversy between 1606 and 1610. For examples, see Blackwell (1609: 41, 54, 55, 131), Donne (1610: 244), James I (1609: 57) and Persons (1608: 78).
7. For an excellent study of James's identification with King Solomon, see Guibbory (2010: 21–55).
8. For Donne's reading of Augustine, see Ettenhuber (2011: 23–64).
9. The source of this story is Paul the Deacon's eighth-century continuation of Eutropius's *Breviarium Historiae Romanae*, printed at Lyons in 1594 (cf. Donne, 1993: 283, 425). The sixth-century Emperor Tiberius II Constantine (520–582) was often praised for his benevolence and charity.
10. For an example of an interpretation of 'Woman's Constancy' that highlights its misogynistic elements, see Canfield (1989: 157–65).

References

Aquinas, Saint Thomas (1947). *Summa Theologica*. Trans. Fathers of the English Dominican Province. *Christian Classics Ethereal Library*. February 2014 <http://www.ccel.org/ccel/aquinas/summa.i.html>.

Augustine of Hippo (1610). *St. Augustine, Of the Citie of God*. Trans. De civitate Dei. Early English Books Online. February 2014.

Blackwell, George (1609). *A Large Examination taken at Lambeth, According to his Maiesties Direction, Point by Point, of M. G. Blakwell, made Arch-priest of England, by Pope Clement 8*. Early English Books Online. February 2014.

Canfield, Douglas J. (1989). *Word as Bond in English Literature from the Middle Ages to the Restoration*. Philadelphia, PA: University of Pennsylvania Press.

Carey, John (1981). *John Donne: Life, Mind and Art*. London: Faber.

Castiglione, Baldesar (1959). *The Book of the Courtier*. Trans. Charles S. Singleton. New York: Anchor Books.

Donne, John (1610). *Pseudo-Martyr Wherein out of certaine propositions and gradations, this conclusion is euicted. That those which are of the Romane religion in this kingdome, may and ought to take the Oath of Allegiance.* London: Printed by W. Stansby for Walter Burre. STC 7048.

Donne, John (1984). *Biathanatos.* Ed. Ernest W. Sullivan. Newark, NY: U of Delaware P; London: Associated UP.

Donne, John (1993). *Pseudo-Martyr: Wherein out of Certain Propositions and Gradations, this Conclusion is Evicted. That those which are of the Roman Religion in this Kingdom, may and ought to Take the Oath of Allegiance.* Ed. Anthony Raspa. Montreal & Kingston, London and Buffalo: McGill-Queen's UP.

Donne, John (2005). *The Variorum Edition of the Poetry of John Donne.* Vol. 7.1. Ed. Gary A. Stringer. Bloomington and Indianapolis: Indiana UP.

Donne, John (2010). *The Complete Poems of John Donne: Epigrams, Verse Letters to Friends, Love-Lyrics, Love-Elegies, Satire, Religion Poems, Wedding Celebrations, Verse Epistles to Patronesses, Commemorations and Anniversaries.* Ed. Robin Robbins. Harlow, New York: Longman.

Ettenhuber, Katrin (2011). *Donne's Augustine: Renaissance Cultures of Interpretation.* Oxford and New York: Oxford UP.

Frost, Kate Gartner (1990). *Holy Delight: Typology, Numerology, and Autobiography in Donne's Devotions Upon Emergent Occasions.* Princeton, New Jersey: Princeton UP.

Guibbory, Achsah (2010). *Christian Identity, Jews, and Israel in Seventeenth-Century England.* Oxford and New York: Oxford UP.

Hadfield, Andrew (forthcoming). 'Chapter Twenty Four: Controversial Prose.' *John Donne in Context.* Ed. Michael Schoenfeldt. Cambridge: Cambridge UP.

James, I King of England (1609). *An Apologie for the Oath of Allegiance. Early English Books Online.* February 2014.

Jay, Martin (2010). *The Virtues of Mendacity: On Lying in Politics.* Charlottesville, VA: U of Virginia P.

Kenyon, J.P. (1986). *The Stuart Constitution, 1603–1688.* 2nd ed. Cambridge: Cambridge UP.

Knott, John R. (2010). *Discourses of Martyrdom in English Literature, 1563–1694.* New York: Cambridge UP.

Lake, Peter and Questier, Michael (2011). *The Trials of Margaret Clitherow: Persecution, Martyrdom and the Politics of Sanctity in Elizabethan England.* London, New York: Continuum Publishing Corporation.

MacDonald, Michael (1989). 'The Medicalization of Suicide in England: Laymen, Physicians, and Cultural Change, 1500–1870.' Vol. 67. *The Milbank Quarterly* suppl. 1: 69–91.

Malloch, A.E. (1962). 'John Donne and the Casuists.' *Studies in English Literature, 1500–1900* 2.1: 57–76.

Norbrook, David (1990). 'The Monarchy of Wit and the Republic of letters.' *Soliciting Interpretation: Literary Theory and Seventeenth-Century English poetry.* Eds Elizabeth D. Harvey and Katherine Eisaman Maus. Chicago and London: University of Chicago Press. 3–36.

North, Marcy L. (2002). 'Anonymity's Subject: James I and the Debate over the Oath of Allegiance.' *New Literary History* 33.2: 215–32. 2014.

Persons, Robert (1580). *A brief discours contayning certayne reasons why Catholiques refuse to goe to church. Written by a learned and vertuous man, to a friend of his in England.*

And dedicated by I.H. to the Queenes most excellent Maiestie. Imprinted at Doway by John Lyon i.e. Greenstreet House Press. STC 19394.

Persons, Robert (1608). *The Judgement of a Catholic English-man: Living in Banishment for his Religion. Early English Books Online.* February 2014.

Questier, Michael (1997). 'Loyalty, Religion and State Power in Early Modern England: English Romanism and the Jacobean Oath Of Allegiance.' *The Historical Journal* 40.2: 311–29.

Questier, Michael (2008). 'Catholic Loyalism in Early Stuart England.' *English Historical Review* CXXIII.504: 1–34.

Ryan, Clarence J. (1942). 'The Jacobean Oath of Allegiance and English Lay Catholics.' *The Catholic Historical Review* 28.2: 159–83.

Silving, Helen (1959). 'The Oath: I.' *Yale Law Journal* 68: 1329–90; 'The Oath: II.' *Yale Law Journal* 68: 1527–77.

Slights, Camille W. (1972). '"To Stand Inquiring Right": The Casuistry of Donne's "Satyre III".' *Studies in English Literature, 1500–1900* 12.1: 85–101.

Slights, Camille W. (1992). *The Casuistical Tradition in Shakespeare, Donne, Herbert and Milton.* Princeton: Princeton UP.

Spurr, John (2004). '"The Strongest Bond of Conscience": Oaths and the Limits of Tolerance in Early Modern England.' *Contexts of Conscience in Early Modern Europe, 1500–1700.* Eds Harold Braun and Edward Vallance. Basingstoke: Palgrave Macmillan.

Valbuena, Olga (2000). 'Casuistry, Martyrdom, and the Allegiance Controversy in Donne's "Pseudo-Martyr".' *Religion & Literature* 32.2: 49–80.

Wiggins, Peter DeSa (2000). *Donne, Castiglione and the Poetry of Courtliness.* Indiana, IN: Indiana UP.

Shanyn Altman is based at the University of Sussex (Centre for Early Modern and Medieval Studies). Her research interests include religious and political toleration in the works of John Donne, casuistry, and martyrdom in the early modern period. She has published on Donne's *Ignatius His Conclave* and the *Devotions.*

Kirsten Sandrock

TRUTH AND LYING IN EARLY MODERN TRAVEL NARRATIVES: CORYAT'S *CRUDITIES*, LITHGOW'S *TOTALL DISCOURSE* AND GENERIC CHANGE

This article looks at concepts of truth and falsehood in early modern travel narratives, focusing particularly on Thomas Coryat's Crudities (1611) and William Lithgow's The Totall Discourse (1614). It argues that these travelogues point towards a change in the generic conventions of literature, especially the split between factual and fictional narratives that emerged in the course of the early modern period and which is decisive for understanding conceptions of mendacity in literary accounts. Partly, the texts by Coryat and Lithgow still cling to long-established practices of myth-making in travel writing; but partly, they already follow new expectations concerning the veracity of travel narratives and, in the case of Coryat, they even use (a simulation of) accuracy for spectacular and satirical effects.

The early modern period saw a significant transformation of the generic conception of travel literature. Whereas medieval travel narratives were still allowed and quite possibly expected to invent parts of their material, this convention changed, at least partly, in the early modern period, when authenticity and truth emerged as new genre standards of travelogues. In this article I suggest that the change of generic conventions coincides with the emergence of two superordinate genres – nowadays usually referred to as 'fiction' and 'nonfiction' – that have long governed understandings of truth and falsehood in literature. I will expand on existing studies of the emergence of factual and fictional works in early modernity by specifically showing how European travel narratives of the period contributed to and reflected upon changing conceptions of veracity and mendacity in literary works.[1] The two texts I look at in detail are Thomas Coryat's *Crudities* (1611) and William Lithgow's *The Totall Discourse* (1614). Using a genre theory approach, I propose that a reading of these travelogues allows us to see how literary conceptions of truth and lying were taking shape in the early seventeenth century, and how the categories 'fiction' and 'nonfiction' were already consciously worked and played with by travel writers of that time.

1. Generic conventions and the maxim of truth

According to David Duff's *Modern Genre Theory* (2000: xiii), literary genres can be defined as 'a recurring type or category of text, as defined by structural, thematic and/or functional criteria'. In the case of travel narratives, the defining generic feature is, surely, their common subject matter: the narration of travel experiences. In addition to this thematic marker, though, the genre of travel writing as we know it today seems to be further characterised by what Martin Steinmann (1981: 243) calls 'superordinate genre conventions'. Steinmann uses this phrase to refer to the conventions readers apply, mostly unconsciously, to the reading and interpretation of texts. In line with our accumulated reading experiences, readers from the Western cultural sphere usually divide texts into two superordinate or meta-genres, namely 'fictional' versus 'nonfictional' narratives (243). While I generally agree with Steinmann's theory in relation to (non-professional) readers today, I would like to suggest that it is necessary to historicise his theory in order to avoid anachronistic applications of the binary paradigm to earlier narratives. Early seventeenth-century travel literature is an ideal starting place for such an investigation, because it is in this period that the genre division between fact and fiction becomes relevant for narrative prose. A brief excursion into genre theory approaches to factional and fictional literature will help to pave the way for this argument and for my reading of Coryat's and Lithgow's texts.

Following Steinmann (1981: 251–2) and communication theorists such as Paul Grice (1989), there are fundamental differences in the ways readers commonly approach fiction and nonfiction. Most important for my purpose are the different expectations readers bring to fictional and nonfictional texts regarding the maxim of truth. In his theory of communication, Grice (1989: 139) identifies the 'truth condition' as one of four principal maxims of successful conversation. In literary studies, this premise of the 'truth condition' has gained ground, amongst others, through the work of empirical critics such as Siegfried J. Schmidt (1982: 47–108). Schmidt argues that readers of fiction are willing to replace the 'fact-convention' of their day-to-day conversations with the so-called 'aesthetic convention' in order to be able to 'participate in aesthetic communication' (51). Steinmann (1981: 252) similarly maintains that the maxim of truth is suspended when readers approach fiction: 'in interpreting a fictional world, we may replace our real beliefs about natural laws and historical facts, the beliefs we use in interpreting nonfictional worlds, with the beliefs that, we have reason to suppose, the writer intended or expected us to have'. The key point is that superordinate genre conventions determine our approach and reaction to the 'truth' of literary texts even before we read them. If readers consider a narrative to be fictional, then they will dispense with the maxim of truth and allow for events to happen that they would otherwise consider untrue, misleading or downright mendacious. If, in contrast, readers expect a narrative to be nonfictional, then they will count on its reliable representation of facts and insist on the accuracy of the narrated events. In other words, fiction allows for the fabrication of facts and regards this fabrication as part of the aesthetic principle, whereas nonfiction treats fabricated facts as mendacity.

Of course, there are exceptions to this clear demarcation. Steinmann (1981: 250) names the historical novel as a hybrid genre that mixes fact and fiction. What he does not do is to ask when and how the meta-generic conventions came into being. Consequently, Steinmann ignores the pre-history of narratives that antedate the generic distinction between fiction and nonfiction. I believe such a historical investigation is necessary in order to comprehend and appreciate not only the generic formations of early modern literatures but also the role that truth and lying play in works of the period. Such an investigation can also benefit from drawing on reception theory, particularly Hans Robert Jauss's model of the reader's 'horizon of expectations' (1970: 12). According to Jauss (2000: 131), the 'horizon of expectations' is linked to the formation of genres in all kinds of communication, influencing not only the ways in which readers approach a text but also the ways in which authors write. The following analysis draws on the idea that readers' expectations have an effect on the development of genres, in this case particularly the expectations concerning the truth value of a text. To illustrate this point, it is useful to briefly review the changes in travel writing from the medieval to the early modern period and to consider these changes in the context of larger cultural events.

2. Early modern travel literature: the evolution of a genre

Between the late fourteenth and the early eighteenth centuries, the generic conventions of travel writing changed fundamentally. In late medieval travel literature, the narration of supernatural events was part of the – unwritten – rules of travel writing. An account such as *The Travels of Sir John Mandeville* (c. 1357–1371) was allowed to invent at least parts of its material, for instance when speaking about an encounter with a man whose daughter is said to have turned 'into likeness of a dragon' (Mandeville, 1983: 9). Consistent with conventions identified by studies of monstrosity in medieval and early modern literature, this example not only illustrates that grotesque figures were commonly located at the outer edges of the world (Ramey, 2008: 84) but also that the female body was often associated with monstrosity.[2] This association will bear on my reading of Lithgow's and Coryat's narratives.

It is to be assumed that late medieval readers and listeners were familiar with fantastic encounters as those included in Mandeville's *Travels* from classical literature such as the *Naturalis Historia* (c. AD 77–79) by Pliny the Elder, where one finds references to monopods (or sciapods), cynocephali (dog-heads) as well as Amazons. Medieval travel authors adapted the classical tradition in their own idiosyncratic manner and frequently narrated encounters with 'demons, non-Christians, the so-called monstrous races, freaks of nature, deformed infants, miscarried fetuses and [...] women' (Miller, 2010: 1). However, in the course of the early modern period, readers' expectations towards the truth value of travel literature changed. We can see this in relation to the reception of George Psalmanazar's *Historical and Geographical Description of Formosa, An Island Subject to the Emperor of Japan. Giving an Account of the Religion, Customs, Manners, etc. of the Inhabitants* of 1704. Psalmanazar had originally claimed that his narrative was a faithful account of Formosa, but when he came to admit that it was fictional – as many readers had suspected all along – he found himself ostracised for what was perceived as literary forgery. If, then, by the early eighteenth century the superordinate genres of fact and fiction had come to inform the reader's horizon of expectations, the question arises as to how and when the maxim of truth became a prevailing principle for readers' approaches to and interpretations of travel literature.

The rise of the new scientific method contributed to the fundamental shift in the general perception of truth, including truth as narrated in literature. Whereas a medieval audience would frequently have been asked to accept the truth of some higher authority – whether religious, worldly or domestic – the early modern period witnessed the emergence of a new consciousness that sought to affirm and test the truth of both old and new knowledges, which included knowledge about foreign countries. The work of scholars and travellers such as Hieronymus Turler (c. 1520–1602), Theodor Zwinger (1533–1588) or Justus Lipsius (1547–1606) contributed to the conception of travelling and travel writing as a scientific practice that was meant to educate both the traveller and the readers of travelogues. In this way, for Francis Bacon in *The New Organon* (1620), travel becomes a model for the benefits of empiricism as a whole: just as 'the regions of the material globe – that is, of the earth, of the sea, and of the stars – have been in our times laid widely open and revealed', so, Bacon argues, 'the intellectual globe should' expand and exceed 'the narrow limits of old discoveries' (Bacon, 1863: Chapter LXXXIV).

In terms of generic developments, the novel conception of travelling as a scientific method is reflected in the rise of a new genre which became prominent in the early modern period: *Ars apodemica* provides precise descriptions of foreign peoples, cultures and places by including lists or detailed reports about the topography, natural products and cultural conventions of the travelled countries. This information was meant to supply future travellers with details about the countries they would visit. In addition, and more critically, *ars apodemica* helped to accumulate information that would significantly help European countries such as England or Spain to establish colonial regimes abroad. Knowledge about foreign cultures became an instrument of power. The genre of the so-called Spanish questionnaires illustrates this point. Spanish colonists frequently conducted surveys in the Americas and passed the information they gathered on to the colonial administration. As Daniel Carey (2009: 167–8) states, the questionnaires were originally devised '[u]nder the aegis of the Council of the Indies (Consejo de Indias)' in order to seek 'wide-ranging information on the natural and moral history of the Americas, as well as the governance of territories under the viceroyalties of New Spain and Peru'. Although the questionnaires were not meant to be published or to be read by a general audience at the time, they were archived by the colonial administration and used to keep a detailed record about the topography and cultural history of the overseas territories. According to Carey, the 'most substantial of these documents proposed several hundred questions inviting a comprehensive survey and ethnography' (168),[3] which illustrates how enormous the appetite of the Spanish colonisers was for information on those parts of the world they sought to dominate.

Even if other forms of travel writing were not quite as systematic as the Spanish questionnaires, the influence of the new scientific method on travel writing, especially the insistence on detailed description and reliability, was substantial and helped to constitute a new approach to the concept of truth in literature. A case in point is the 'Prologue to the Reader' from Lithgow's *The Totall Discourse* (1614), which will be analysed in more detail below. Here, the narrator guarantees that everything he reports is based on eye-witness experiences, which may well be read as a response to readers' growing demand for factuality:

> This laborious worke then of mine, depending on this preamble, is onely composed of mine owne eye sight, and occular experience (pluris est occulatus testis unus, quam auriti decem). To the wise I know it will be welcome, to the profound Historian, yeeld knowledge, contemplation, and direction, and to the understanding Gentlemen, insight, instruction, and recreation.
>
> (Lithgow, 2005: 19)

Veracity here simply means the report of first-hand experiences, which says nothing about the actual truthfulness of the account, but which offers insight into the concept of truth that was being promoted in early modern travelogues. Lennard J. Davis (1991) makes a similar point with regard to narratives of New World explorers. According to Davis (1991: 243), it is not clear what 'the climate of factuality' in these narratives was. Many of their alleged discoveries and truthful accounts were either based on second-hand material or, indeed, on invented, i.e. fictional, stories.

As for Lithgow, I would not go so far as to say that his entire account is invented. My later reading will illustrate that *The Totall Discourse* may have bent the truth at times, but what is important for now is that the text's insistence on its status as an eye-witness account and, hence, its supposed reliability was so central to the narrative that it was made plain in the prologue to the reader. In this manner, the passage is indicative of what Davis (1983: 67) has termed the 'news/ novels discourse' in early modern literature, which is marked by 'an insistence on recentness as well as on factuality'. As Davis notes (70), this insistence did not mean that the texts always *were* recent or factual; but many authors proclaimed these qualities to be properties of their work, which demonstrates that concepts of newness and factuality were becoming governing principles of some literary accounts, including travel writing. In the case of Lithgow's prologue, such an understanding of truthfulness is correlated with the idea of the travelogue as a source of edification. The narrator stresses that his account will benefit his audience because its truthfulness will instruct them about the world.

The emphasis on the facticity of Lithgow's narrative also emerges in other formal features, such as the first-person narrative of the account, as well as in thematic conventions that Jonathan P.A. Sell (2012: 227) calls 'truth topics'. In his article 'Embodying Truth in Early Modern English Travel Writing', Sell discusses the formal and thematic means by which the concept of truth was conveyed in travelogues of the period. A central example of such a truth topic is the literary representation of the travel writers' bodies, which were frequently marked by the exhaustion of their travels as evidence for the genuineness of their experiences (227–41). In Lithgow's *Totall Discourse*, the use of body imagery emerges most prominently in two respects: first, in the narrator's repeated insistence on his travels by foot, and, second, in his account of the physical pain he has to endure after being caught by the Spanish Inquisition (Sell, 2012: 234–7). A passage about his torture in Spain will serve as an example of how the narrativised body is used as a rhetorical strategy to mark the authenticity of the traveller's experiences:

> Now mine eyes begun to startle, my mouth to foame and froath, and my teeth to chatter like to the doubling of Drummers stickes. O strange inhumanity of Menmonster Manglers! surpassing the limits of their nationall Law; three score Tortures beeing the tryall of Treason, which I had, and was to indure: yet thus to inflict a seaven-fold surplussage of more intollerable cruelties: And notwithstanding of my shivering lippes, in this fiery passion my vehement groaning, and blood-springing fonts, from armes, broke sinewes, hammes, and knees; yea, and my depending weight on flesh-cutting Cords; yet they stroke mee on the face with Cudgels, to abate and cease the thundring noyse of my wrestling voyce.
>
> (Lithgow, 2005: 271)

The passage illustrates how, in Lithgow's narrative, 'travel writing thus becomes the literal anatomy of secular martyrdom' (Sell, 2012: 234). Moreover, a reading of the scene in the light of the text's truth value suggests that the tortured body is used as a motif to authenticate the report's faithfulness. And yet, I want to suggest that Lithgow's detailed description of his bodily pains works as a two-sided rhetorical strategy. On the surface, it may function as a 'truth topic', as it was certainly intended to convince contemporary readers of his uprightness, both as a Protestant who will not bow to the Spanish Inquisition, and as a traveller who avoids no pains to tell readers what is going on in the world. Yet, knowing Lithgow's inclination towards hyperbole, for which further examples will be given below, one might easily call into question the reliability of the account or, at least, wonder about the odds of exaggeration. It is, of course, impossible to prove either the truth or the falseness of this passage, and there is no need to try. What is important is that the narration of facts and the fabrication of fictional events were still very close in early modern travel writing.

On the one hand, the new scientific method established truthfulness as a marker of factual writing, but on the other hand, an early modern audience supposedly still expected the inclusion of extraordinary or supernatural events in travel narratives of the period. Indeed, there were good reasons to draw on the earlier tradition of relating supernatural events in travel writing, as Stephen Greenblatt (1991) demonstrates in *Marvellous Possessions*. According to Greenblatt, the fantastic was a central feature in New World travel narratives of the period not despite but, rather, because of the fact that explorers wanted to convey new 'truths'. In such works, the fantastic is no longer used to explain the world, but it is increasingly used as a means to help readers come to terms with the existence of newness in the world:

> The marvellous is a central feature [...] in the whole complex system of representation, verbal and visual, philosophical and aesthetic, intellectual and emotional, through which people in the late Middle Ages and the Renaissance apprehended, and thence possessed or discarded, the unfamiliar, the alien, the terrible, the desirable and the hateful.
>
> (Greenblatt, 1991: 22–3)

It is useful to keep this argument in mind when examining the concepts of truth and lying in the narratives by Lithgow and Coryat. Greenblatt's conception of the marvellous might help to explain why these travel narratives did not fully discard the earlier convention of myth-making even if they otherwise claimed to abide by the maxim of truth.

And yet, in the following I wish to argue that the cognitive function as suggested by Greenblatt was not the only reason why the marvellous remained a central feature in early modern travel accounts. In addition to speaking about newness in the world, it also served a much simpler function, namely to make travel accounts more attractive to the readership. Lithgow's *The Totall Discourse* (1614) and Coryat's *Crudities* (1611) evoke these various functions of the narration of supernatural or extraordinary events in different manners. While *The Totall Discourse* clings to the practices of myth-making in a way that illustrates the persistence of the readers' 'horizons of expectations' from earlier travel narratives, Coryat's *Crudities* adopts a more complex narrative strategy. His account superficially fulfils the readers' demand for new information and accuracy, but actually the text only uses this demand to include spectacular events that would otherwise be problematic to tell in a factual travel account. In this manner, Coryat's narrative not only plays with the emerging truth convention; it may even be an early satirical comment on it, as we will see below.

3. Lithgow's *The Totall Discourse*

William Lithgow (*c.* 1582–1645) was born *c.* 1582 in Lanark in southern Scotland and died sometime in or after 1645 (Garrett, 2004). According to Clifford Bosworth (2006: 17), he was probably 'educated at Lanark Grammar School' and 'clearly received [...] a solid classical education plus a knowledge of the Bible and catechisms'. Apart from this, Lithgow did not seem to belong to the upper classes. At least, he practised a 'distinctly un-aristocratic mode of travel' that saw him voyaging on foot, rather than on horses or other animals (4). Lithgow's first voyage led him to continental Europe, northern Africa and the Middle East. Later on, Lithgow also travelled to Ireland and Spain, where he claimed that he was tortured by the Spanish Inquisition.

The experiences of Lithgow's travels are set down in *The Totall Discourse of the Rare Adventures and Painefull Peregrinations of Long Nineteene Years Travayles from Scotland to the most Kingdoms in Europe, Asia and Affrica.* The narrative was first published in abridged form in 1614 and quickly became so popular that it was followed by a second, equally successful edition in 1616 (Lawrence, 2005: 10). Since then, the text has gone through numerous editions and has turned into one of the most widely read travel narratives in Europe. In 2009, a German translation of *The Totall Discourse* was published as *Die wundersamen Irrfahrten des William Lithgow*, which roughly translates as 'The Wondrous Odyssey of William Lithgow'. The title of the German translation plays with the widespread image of Lithgow as a rover, whose travels were full of naivety and folly, if not outright fabrication. In fact, fantastic episodes play a central role in Lithgow's narrative, as I shall demonstrate below. But, at the same time, *The Totall Discourse* echoes the demand for authenticity and truth in early modern travel writing. From the opening passages of the text, the narrator stresses the veracity of his experiences, stating that 'this worke [is] being fensed with experience, and garnished with trueth' (Lithgow, 2005: 19). The idea behind this proclamation was that the text could contribute to the edification of its readers. As Theo van Heijnsbergen (2010: 227) puts it, 'Lithgow developed a philosophy of travel as *Selbstbildung*' – meaning a holistic 'self-education' through independent studies – in which not only travelling itself but also the reading of travel writing is presented as part of the humanist ideal for which, as we have seen, Bacon saw travel as a paradigm.

In *The Totall Discourse*, the understanding of travel writing as a source of knowledge acquisition becomes clear in a section in which the author addresses his book as if it were a teacher to the (imagined) readership:

> Instruct the Curious, inlarge the Servile Mind,
> Illuminate misunderstandings blinde:
> Sound Knowledge in their ears, deigne to approove me,
> Since Friends and Foes, the World and I, must love thee.
>
> (Lithgow, 2005: 21)

In these lines, Lithgow claims that by publishing his travel experiences, he seeks to pass his knowledge on to others. He forges a link between *The Totall Discourse* and *ars apodemica* literature which informs the entire narrative, both in content and style. Apart from explicit statements about his purpose of writing the travelogue, the influence of the new scientific method emerges in those parts of the text that provide detailed descriptions of distant countries. For instance, the narrator describes places such as Greece, the Aegean Islands or Constantinople in a style that evokes *ars apodemica* – such as in the meticulous listing of typical foods and detailed description of the landscape. Here is an example of Lithgow's account of Crete:

> Dates, Figges, Orenges, Lemmons, and Pomi del Adamo growing all through other; And at the rootes of which trees grew Wheate, Malmsie, Muscadine, Leaticke, Wines, Grenadiers, Carnobiers, Mellones, and all other sorts of fruites and hearbes, the earth can yeeld to man …
>
> (63)

Through its cataloguing of the island's natural produce, Lithgow's narrative reflects the early modern demand for specific information and systematic descriptions. The detailed description of the fruit and other edible plants on the island would allow readers back home to gain a sense of place and, for future travellers, to know what to expect on Crete in agricultural terms.

Yet, if certain parts of *The Totall Discourse* can be linked to *ars apodemica*, then other parts indicate that it is still influenced by the more fabulous conventions of classical and medieval travel literature. There are sections of the narrative that call into question, for the modern reader at least, the veracity of the account and are more reminiscent of Pliny than they are of the maxim of truth. In Berne, for instance, Lithgow (200) gives a report of a woman who had allegedly not eaten or drunk anything for 13 years. Admittedly, he does not say that he met the woman; but the mere inclusion of the legend in his narrative betrays Lithgow's desire for embellishing his text with fantastic stories. The same desire for making his narrative more extraordinary, and, arguably, more interesting for the reader can be seen in an account of the protagonist's travels on the Isle of Lesina. The narrator states that a Venetian governor invited him to see 'some marvellous misshapen creature borne in the Iland' (45). Naturally, the narrator accepts. He goes to the house of the so-called 'Monster' and describes the encounter in fabulous terms. It is worth quoting the passage in full, because it brings out Lithgow's keenness to include fantastic elements in his narrative, despite his earlier insistence on the travelogue's educational purpose:

> Which unnaturall Childe being brought, I was amazed in that sight, to behold the deformity of Nature; for below the middle part, there was but one body, and above the middle there was two living soules, each one separated from another with severall members. Their heads were both of one bignesse but different in Phisnomy: The belly and their faces looked both one way, as if the one had carried the other on his backe, and often before our eyes he that was behind, would lay his hands about the necke of the foremost. Their eyes were exceeding bigge, and their hands greater then an Infant of three times their age. The excrements of both creatures issued foorth at one place, and their thighes and legges of a great growth, not semblable to their age, being but sixe and thirty dayes old; and their feete were proportionably made like to the foot of Cammell, round and cloven in the middest. They received their food with an insatiable desire, and continually mourned with a pitifull noyse; that sorrowfull man told us, that when the one slept, the other awaked, which was a strange disagreement in Nature.
>
> (46)

The narrative here shows a desire to make a story more spectacular by means of hyperbole. It may well be that Lithgow actually did encounter conjoined twins on the Isle of Lesina whose sight he may have found startling. Yet, the declaration that the children's feet 'were proportionably made like to the foot of Cammell' is highly unlikely, as is the statement that their 'hands' were actually 'three times' greater than normal (46). *The Totall Discourse* wallows in the alleged monstrosity of the children on the Isle of Lesina, thereby using a strategy that is reminiscent of the Mandeville example above. In both cases the monstrous body is located in a topographically remote place and in both cases it is compared with the body of a foreign or a fantastic animal – a dragon in Mandeville's text and a camel in Lithgow's case – to highlight their allegedly nonhuman status.

There is no way to prove how much of Lithgow's narrative is made up, and there is no need for such a proof, because, as I have been arguing, it would be anachronistic to classify early modern travelogues along the binary lines of fictional versus nonfictional literature. *The Totall Discourse* displays the tenacity of older conventions of travel writing despite the fact that it openly claims to abide by the maxim of truth. It is likely that Lithgow included such stories as the one of the conjoined twins to make his text more alluring to a broad audience. As Ingo

Berensmeyer states with regard to the changing forms and functions of literature in the early modern period:

> The media change around 1500 conditions a fundamentally new structure of communication situations, because the printed book is geared toward an audience that may be and probably will be much more diffuse than that of a speaker who addresses a gathering of listeners.
>
> (Berensmeyer, 2004: 629)

Lithgow was, in all probability, aware of this new diversity of his readership, especially since he seems to have been unpaid for his travels and may therefore have been dependent on the revenues of his publications. In fact, there is evidence that Lithgow consciously thought about his audience when writing his text. He singles out the 'wise', the 'Historian' and 'the understanding Gentlemen' as anticipated readers of his account (Lithgow, 2005: 19). And yet, it is likely that Lithgow sought to make the narrative appeal not only to this limited group but to all kinds of readers, including those who are seeking factual information and those who enjoy more truth-bending anecdotes.

4. Coryat's *Crudities*

I turn to my second example, Thomas Coryat's *Crudities*, which will show how early seventeenth-century travel narratives were not only aware of existing and emerging genre conventions but how they sometimes openly played with them and used them for humorous, perhaps even satirical effect. The first volume of *Coryat's Crudities* was published in 1611. The author, Thomas Coryat (*c*. 1577–1617) – also spelled Coryate – was educated at Winchester and Oxford. In 1608, he embarked on his travels to continental Europe, especially central and southern Europe, which he described in, to give it its full title, *Coryat's Crudities: Hastily gobled up in five Moneths travells in France, Savoy, Italy, Rhetia commonly called the Orisons country, Helvetia alias Switzerland, some parts of high Germany and the Nether lands; Newly digested in the hungry aire of Odcombe in the County of Somerset, and now dispersed to the nourishment of the travelling Members of this Kingdome.*[4]

The title gives reason to pause. The word 'crudities' was, in the early modern period, mostly associated with digestion problems. In this way, the title adds another facet to the previously introduced idea that early modern travellers sought to validate the truthfulness of their accounts, amongst others, by means of bodily descriptions. In the words of Katharine Craik (2004: 80), writing about *Coryat's Crudities*, the 'metaphor of crudity is judiciously chosen, for the art of good digestion is often emphasized in writings of and about travelers at the turn of the seventeenth century'. In addition, it can be argued that the title's metaphor heralds the humorous and sometimes self-ironic tone of the narrative, which will be central to my argument below.

Coryat's Crudities is written in a personalised mode of narration and stresses the unconventional nature of the author's travels. At the same time, it provides detailed descriptions of the places Coryat visits and thereby adapts to the new educational dictum of early modern travelogues. According to Andrew Hadfield (1998: 66), *Coryat's Crudities* 'is a departure in English travel writing' because of its 'rambling form' and 'the eccentric persona who holds the narrative together' and keeps 'the reader's interest beyond the worth of the material represented'. More-over, the authorial persona, I suggest, repeatedly plays with the maxim of truth. It does so in a rhetorically more complex manner than Lithgow's narrative, because *Coryat's Crudities* mocks the new maxim of veracity by explicitly using it to include information that one would not expect to find in allegedly educational literature. As an illustration, I would like to look at the courtesan episode, which is part of Coryat's account of Venice.

After describing the city in some architectural and cultural detail, the text recounts Coryat's encounter with a Venetian courtesan. The depiction of the pecu-liarity of this woman is reminiscent of the episodes featuring extraordinary females in Mandeville's text. The difference is that the curiousness of the Venetian courte-san no longer lies in her monstrosity but instead in her extraordinary beauty and, arguably, in her sexuality. Accordingly, the literary scene begins with some mythi-cal comparisons to erotically charged women from classical literature. The narrator depicts the courtesans' splendour by using images such as 'amorous Calypsoes' to invoke their legendary beauty, and comparing their habitat with 'the Paradise of Venus' (Coryat, 1905: 403). The allusions to Greek and Latin literature not only conjure up ideas of love and sexuality but, in the case of the Greek Calypso, also pick up earlier traditions of classical travel literature, in this case Homer's *Odyssey*. Following these mythological descriptions of the Venetian women, the narrator claims that he spoke with the courtesans, but that he had no physical contact with any of them. He then sets out to claim the veracity of his account with the following words:

> And I have here inserted a picture of one of their nobler Cortezans, according to her Venetian habites, with my owne neare unto her, made in that forme as we saluted each other. Surely by so much the more willing I am to treat something of them, because I per ceive it is so rare a matter to find a descrip-tion of the Venetian Cortezans in any Authour, that all the writers that I could ever see, which have described the city, have altogether excluded them out of their writings.
>
> (401)

The text here emphasises the informative value of the travel narrative, with the narrator taking pride in presenting an account of the courtesans to his readers that no other travelogue has treated so far. By this means, the text brings together two seemingly contradictory paradigms: the fantastical and the factual. The former materialises in references to classical literature and their connotations of sexual seduction, whereas the latter comes out in the inclusion of the drawing that, alleg-edly, depicts the narrator with the Venetian courtesan in the exact same manner as they met each other.

The combination of the two narrative frames – the truthful and the fantastic – has a rather comic effect on the narrative. It appears, at least to this reader, as if Coryat only invokes the lack of existing accounts of Venetian courtesans in order to be able to feature this flamboyant episode in his own account. In other words, *Coryat's Crudities* exploits the convention of truthfulness for the sake of adding literary glamour to the account. One can even go further and read the courtesan episode as an early example of satirising the genre conventions of authenticity and truthfulness in early modern travel narratives. Indeed, the satirical quality of Coryat's courtesan episode was picked up upon by contemporary readers. The panegyric verses preceding the text testify as much. Apparently, Coryat 'solicit [ed]' these traditional verses of praise himself 'for his publication' by circulating copies of the travelogue before its official publication (Strachan, 2004). Yet, what was meant to strengthen the appeal of his work turned out to be a dubious gift from the roughly 'sixty contributors', among them 'many illustrious authors' but also anonymous contributors (Strachan, 2004). One nameless author satirises the narrator's insistence on his virtuous behaviour with the courtesan in Venice, thereby openly calling into question whether the episode abides by the maxim of truth:

> More sweet in Venice towne there was,
> That wisht him for her owne:
> But shee could never him hand fast;
> For as a Gelding he was chast,
> Though Gelding he were none.

> (Coryat, 1905: 24)

Using animal metaphors for absent sexual relations, the panegyric verse mocks the traveller's alleged purity in Venice. The quotation questions the authenticity of the account and puts forward the charge that the author may have strayed from the truth quite a bit. Quite possibly, the anonymous author picks up on the narrative's own satirical tone, which stretches from the humorous title of the book to its ironic allusion to the truth convention as a reason for including the courtesan episode. Following Craik's (2004: 86) argument that '*Crudities* resembles Menippean satire' with its typical 'mix [of] fact with fantasy', the courtesan episode can be read as an example of the ways in which Coryat's *Crudities* consciously plays with the newly arising conventions of travel literature, especially its maxim of truthfulness, in order to make the narrative both more eccentric and, generically speaking, more self-reflexive.

5. Conclusion

Both Coryat's *Crudities* and Lithgow's *Totall Discourse* were written at a time when the superordinate genres of fiction and nonfiction became increasingly important markers for readers' approaches to literature. A genre theory approach to these texts demonstrates that authors of the period were already conscious of the relatively new convention that travel literature was supposed to be factual and informative. At the same time, the recurrent incorporation of exaggerated or unlikely travel episodes corroborates that these genre conventions were not yet fully superimposed on early seventeenth-century travelogues. It was still possible to rope in fantastic or at least extraordinary encounters either to fulfil readers' expectations, as in the case of Lithgow, or to play with the idea of truthfulness in order to make the narrative more glamorous and, at the same time, more satirical, as in the case of *Coryat's Crudities*.

In the end, then, it is clear that Steinmann's theory of two superordinate genres that determine our understanding of truth and lying in literature needs to be qualified and, in some cases, revised with regard to the period a text was written in. For the early modern age, the question is not whether travelogues were telling the truth or whether they were lying. My reading illustrates that early modern travel accounts were not yet judged solely on account of their truthfulness, even if the authors repeatedly claim the veracity of their account and thereby attest to the growing importance of this generic convention. It was only in the second half of the seventeenth century that '[p]eople's opinion and careers [...] hung on the interpretation given to their writing' with regard to the maxim of truthfulness (Davis, 1983: 150). In the early seventeenth century, the generic conventions of travel literature still allowed, perhaps encouraged and quite possibly required, the telling of episodes that would later on be considered fictional.

With regard to our own age, the question is why many readers continue to abide by such superordinate genre conventions as fictionality versus factuality even if literary practices do not always coincide with such binary schemes. They did not do so in the early modern period and they also do not do so in other literary periods and genres, ranging from the historical novel to postmodern fiction, life writing and postcolonial literature, to name but a few. Literatures from all of these periods and types call into question conventional understandings of fact and fiction and, in so doing, complicate any simple definition of mendacity in literature.

Acknowledgements

Earlier versions of this article were presented at the conference 'History in Travel Narrative 1589–1826' in Paris in 2010 and at the seminar 'Early Modern Constructions of Europe' at the conference of The International Comparative Literature Association in Paris in 2013. I would like to thank the organisers and participants of both conferences/seminars for their input and suggestions.

Disclosure statement

No potential conflict of interest was reported by the author.

Notes

1. See, above all, Davis (1983) and (1991).
2. For a detailed study of the relationship between monstrosity and gender, see Miller (2010).

3. For the original documents, see de Solano (1988).
4. Several years after the publication of his first travelogue, Coryat departed for another journey to Greece, the eastern Mediterranean countries, Persia and Mughal India. He died on his second voyage in 1617.

References

Bacon, Francis (1863). 'The New Organon; Or True Directions Concerning the Interpretation of Nature.' [1620]. Trans. James Spedding, Robert Leslie Ellis and Douglas Denon Heath. *The Works of Francis Bacon*. Vol. VIII. Boston, MA: Taggard and Thompson.

Berensmeyer, Ingo (2004). 'No Fixed Address: Pascal, Cervantes, and the Changing Function of Literary Communication in Early Modern Europe.' *New Literary History* 34: 623–37.

Bosworth, Clifford Edmund (2006). *An Intrepid Scot: William Lithgow of Lanark's Travels into the Ottoman Lands, North Africa and Central Europe, 1609–21*. Aldershot: Ashgate.

Carey, Daniel (2009). 'Hakluyt's Instructions: The Principal Navigations and Sixteenth-century Travel Advice.' *Studies in Travel Writing* 13.2: 167–85.

Coryat, Thomas (1905). *Coryat's Crudities: Hastily Gobled up in Five Moneths Travells in France, Savoy, Italy, Rhetia Commonly Called the Orisons Country, Helvetia Alias Switzerland, Some Parts of High Germany and the Nether Lands; Newly Digested in the Hungry Aire of Odcombe in the County of Somerset, and Now Dispersed to the Nourishment of the Travelling Members of this Kingdome*. [1611]. 2 vols. Glasgow: MacLehose and Sons. Repr. Toronto: Centre for Reformation and Renaissance Studies. 28 February 2010. Web.

Craik, Katharine A. (2004). 'Reading *Coryat's Crudities* [1611].' *Studies in English Literature* 44: 77–96.

Davis, Lennard J. (1983). *Factual Fictions: The Origins of the English Novel*. New York: Columbia University Press.

Davis, Lennard J. (1991). 'The Fact of Events and the Event of Facts: New World Explorers and the Early Novel.' *The Eighteenth Century* 32.3: 240–55.

Duff, David (2000). *Modern Genre Theory*. Ed. David Duff. Edinburgh: Pearson Education.

Garrett, Martin (2004). 'Lithgow, William.' *Oxford Dictionary of National Biography*. Eds H.C.G. Matthew and Brian Harrison. Oxford: OUP. 8 October 2014. <http://www.oxforddnb.com.oxforddictionaryofnationalbiography.han.sub.uni-goettingen.de/view/article/16774?docPos=4>.

Greenblatt, Stephen (1991). *Marvellous Possessions: The Wonder of the New World*. Oxford: Clarendon Press.

Grice, Paul (1989). *Studies in the Way of Words*. Cambridge: Harvard University Press.

Hadfield, Andrew (1998). *Literature, Travel, and Colonial Writing in the English Renaissance, 1545–1625*. Oxford: Oxford University Press.

Heijnsbergen, Theo van (2010). 'William Lithgow's "Fierce Castalian Veine": Travel Writing and the Re-Location of Identity.' *The Apparelling of Truth: Literature and Literary Culture in the Reign of James VI. A Festschrift for Roderick J. Lyall*. Eds Kevin J. McGinley and Nicola Royan. Cambridge: Cambridge Scholars Publishing. 223–40.

Jauss, Hans Robert (1970). 'Literary History as a Challenge to Literary Theory.' *New Literary History* 2.1: 7–37.

Jauss, Hans Robert (2000). 'Theories of Genres in Medieval Literature.' *Modern Genre Theory*. Ed. David Duff. Edinburgh: Pearson Education. 127–47.

Lawrence, B.I. (2005). *Introduction. Rare Adventures and Painful Peregrinations. By William Lithgow.* New York: Cosimo Classics. 9–15.

Lithgow, William (2005). *The Totall Discourse of the Rare Adventures and Painefull Peregrinations of Long Nineteene Years Travayles from Scotland to the most Kingdoms in Europe, Asia and Affrica.* [1614]. New York: Cosimo Classics.

Lithgow, William (2009). *Die wundersamen Irrfahrten des William Lithgow.* [The Wondrous Odyssey of William Lithgow.] Ed. Roger Willemsen. Trans. Georg Deggerich. Hamburg: Mare.

Mandeville, John (1983). *The Travels of Sir John Mandeville.* [c. 1357–1371]. London: J. Osborne and James Hodges, 1730; Repr. Woodbridge: Research Publications. 12 March 2014. Project Gutenberg. Web.

Miller, Sarah Alison (2010). *Medieval Monstrosity and the Female Body.* New York: Routledge.

Ramey, Lynn Tarte (2008). 'Monstrous Alterity in Early Modern Travel Accounts: Lessons from the Ambiguous Medieval Discourse of Humanness.' *L'Esprit Créateur* 48.1: 81–95.

Schmidt, Siegfried J. (1982). *Foundations for the Empirical Study of Literature: The Components of a Basic Theory.* Trans. Robert de Beaugrande. Papiere zur Textlinguistik 36 / Papers in Textlinguistics 36. Hamburg: Helmut Buske Verlag.

Sell, Jonathan P.A. (2012). 'Embodying truth in early modern English travel writing.' *Studies in Travel Writing* 16.3: 227–41.

de Solano, Francisco, ed. (1988). *Cuestionarios para la formación de la Relaciones Geograficas de Indias siglos XVI/XIX.* [Questionnaires about the Forming of Geographical Relations in the Indies, 16th–19th Centuries.] Madrid: Consejo Superior de Investigaciones Científicas.

Steinmann Jr., Martin (1981). 'Superordinate Genre Conventions.' *Poetics* 10: 243–61.

Strachan, Michael (2004). 'Coryate, Thomas.' *Oxford Dictionary of National Biography.* Eds H.C.G. Matthew and Brian Harrison. Oxford: OUP. 8 October 2014 <http://www.oxforddnb.com.oxforddictionaryofnationalbiography.han.sub.uni-goettingen.de/view/article/6364?docPos=2>.

Kirsten Sandrock is Assistant Professor at the Department for English Literature and Cultural Studies at the Georg-August University Goettingen, Germany. Her research interests range from early modern literature to postcolonial studies, with a special focus on Canadian literature and Scottish studies. Her publications include the monograph *Gender and Region: Maritime Fiction in English by Canadian Women, 1976–2005* (2009) as well as the articles 'The Quest for Authenticity: History and Class in Ian Rankin's Rebus Novels' (*Scottish Literary Review* 3.1 [2011]) and 'Rethinking the Region in Canadian Postcolonial Studies' (*Zeitschrift für Kanada-Studien* 31.2 [2011]). She also co-edited the essay collection with Owain Wright, *Locating Italy: East and West in British–Italian Transactions* (Amsterdam: Rodopi, 2013) and, with Wolfram Keller and J. Derrick McClure, the *EJES* special issue on Scottish Renaissances (18.1 [2014]).

Anne-Julia Zwierlein

'BETRAYED MY CREDULOUS INNOCENCE': MENDACITY AND FEMALE EDUCATION IN JOHN MILTON AND THE 'BATTLE OF THE SEXES'

Using the parallel temptation scenes involving Uriel and Eve in Paradise Lost *and the Lady in* Comus *as case studies, this essay examines the treatment of evil mendacity and virtuous resistance in John Milton. It highlights Milton's engagement with two specific cultural and epistemological contexts: firstly, the Baconian new science and epistemology, and secondly, the 'Battle of the Sexes', a seventeenth-century pamphlet war whose female participants defended women as virtuous and demanded female education. The author argues that, despite the poet's denigration of Eve's fallen feminism in* Paradise Lost, *there are important philosophical alignments between Milton's Baconianism and the philosophy of education as proposed by the female pamphleteers of the 'querelle des femmes'.*

Discourses and practices of mendacity are present on multiple levels in the work of John Milton, most notably in *A Masque Presented at Ludlow Castle* or *Comus* (1634/37) and his epics *Paradise Lost* (1667/74) and *Paradise Regained* (1671). Milton's aristocratic masque about temptation and virtuous resistance centres around the pagan enchanter Comus and his victim, the innocent 'Lady', who is initially deceived and abducted. Although mentally resisting, she is imprisoned in an enchanted chair, '[i]n stony fetters fixed, and motionless' (l. 818). Like *Comus*, both *Paradise Lost* and *Paradise Regained* are interested in the complex question of how the inherently virtuous (the archangels, Christ) or the innocent (the Lady, prelapsarian Adam and Eve) could possibly distinguish between truth and falsehood and withstand strategies of deception. Focused on the figure of Satan, the 'false dissembler', 'fraudulent imposter' and 'guileful tempter' (*PL* 3.681, 692; 9.567), both epics are engaged in debating the knotty questions of theodicy and free will. They depict Satan's deceit (like Comus's) as operating in the realms of both visuality and rhetoric: Satan's frequent metamorphic shape-shifting and guileful rhetoric are mirror images of each other. Both epics also adopt a conflicted stance towards the 'nature' of truth and lying, distinguishing between the eternal, unmovable paradigm of divine truth on the one hand and the situated, historical condition of human agents on the other. Among humans, they insist, the reliability of truth codes has to be negotiated in dialogue with interlocutors.

An example of divine truth is offered in Christ's (privileged) firm resistance to Satan's rather helpless deceptions in *Paradise Regained*, anticipated by Abdiel's opposition to Satan's warmongering in *Paradise Lost*. In accordance with the rules for the allegorical narrative of the *psychomachia* ('battle of the souls'), here the positions of the metaphysical contestants, and the outcome, are clear from the start: 'So spake Israel's true King, and to the Fiend/Made answer meet, that made void all his wiles. /So fares it when with truth falsehood contends' (*PR* 3.441–3). However, the case is more complicated in *Comus* and *Paradise Lost*. Both texts can be taken as exemplifying Milton's insistence on the learning process that is needed for the virtuous and innocent to fend off mendacity. In *Areopagitica* (1644), Milton insists that 'that which purifies us is trial, and trial is by what is contrary' (*CPW* 2: 515): in a fallen world, the innocent have to be exposed to temptation and mendacity in order to learn to distinguish between good and evil and lose their initial gullibility.

The question of learning and education will therefore be central to this essay's inquiry into Milton's treatment of mendacity and resistance. Central case studies will be the parallel temptation scenes involving Uriel and Eve in *Paradise Lost* and the Lady in *Comus*. Looking at the close connections between the Satanic figures' uses of disguise and deceitful speech, the essay argues that the ideological function of these visual deceptions and rhetorical sophistries can be prised open most effectively by attending to the dynamic dialogue between two specific cultural and epistemological contexts. The first is the Baconian new science with its tenet of *veritas filia temporis* ('truth is the daughter of time'), which Catherine Gimelli Martin, Karen Edwards, Angelica Duran and others have identified as highly relevant for Milton's own epistemology (see Edwards, 1999; Duran, 2005; Martin, 2007; 2010). The second is the 'Battle of the Sexes' or *querelle des femmes*, a seventeenth-century pamphlet war about the virtue and value of women (see Woodbridge, 1984; Beilin, 1987; Lewalski, 1993; Miller, 2008; Travitsky and Lake Prescott, 2007–2008). This essay will show that the *querelle*, which was also to a great extent a struggle for female education, dovetails with the Baconian enterprise in surprising ways: both discourses share an insistence on a secularising, experimental scepticism and systematic education. They share a conviction that through education, the effects of the fall, irreversible postlapsarian corruption, can be redressed or at least mitigated. In Milton, femininity is depicted in ambivalent terms: ideas about Eve's innocent gullibility, 'original righteousness' and Baconian questioning spirit are part of Milton's story of the fall. Yet there are also intimations of her feminine, unruly, 'eager appetite' (*PL* 9.740). I will examine how throughout the 'Battle of the Sexes', female pamphleteers addressed both sides of this ambivalent Eve figure. On the one hand, 'many women took pains', as Elaine Beilin claims, 'to emphasize … that women, far from inheriting Eve's penchant for rebellion, were determined to redeem her through virtuous words and deeds' (1987: xiv), thus attempting to rewrite the cultural discourse connecting femininity, sin and corruption. On the other hand, Eve's prelapsarian innocence served as a proto-feminist defence (i.e. not knowing what lies were, Eve had no sensorium for lies).

By juxtaposing the perspectives of Baconianism and the 'Battle of the Sexes', this essay sheds new light on specific seventeenth-century epistemologies of 'truth' and 'falsehood'. It argues that *Comus*, with its Lady figure who learns quickly and adapts well to a challenging situation, offers an example of Milton's utopian commitment to the power of learning and educated reason, comparable to his vision in *Of Education* (1644). Indeed, Rachel Speght, one of the seventeenth-century female pamphleteers, has her allegorical 'Truth' figure cite St Paul's statement that both men and women possess the faculties of 'the mind, the will, the power', and that women's intellect must have been intended by God 'for use' (Speght, 1621: 5). Yet concentrating on the texts' gender politics in relation to their treatment of mendacity and educated resistance can also help us to highlight the differences between Milton's earlier and later treatments of the topic. *Paradise Lost* shows with Eve a more ambivalent figure, held back from pursuing her Baconian scepticism by female sensuousness. In their ways of dealing with mendacity, both Baconianism and proto-feminism reveal the political potential implicit in ideas about returning to a prelapsarian state. For both discourses, the question of education was central. Yet the issue became more radical politically when proto-feminist writers re-employed Baconian epistemological and religious arguments: their strategy enabled them to demand female education as a prerequisite for redeeming the fall. Rather than reiterating the traditional idea of feminine corruption, they claimed that had Eve been better educated, the fall would never have taken place: she would have seen through Satan's disguise and mendacious rhetoric. As this essay will show, despite the poet's denigration of Eve's fallen feminism in *Paradise Lost*, there are important philosophical alignments between Milton's Baconianism and the philosophy of education as proposed by the female pamphleteers of the *querelle des femmes*.

Paradise Lost: the gullibility of innocence

Bacon and Milton locate their philosophical investigations within the circumscription of a fallen state. Engaging with Bacon's famous utopian project that envisages an overturning of the 'idols', the prejudices and false judgements that cloud humanity's perception and thinking (Bacon, 1620: 347), Milton, too, discusses the question of a postlapsarian deficiency of the senses and human understanding – as well as potential remedies. For Baconians, a secular science which assumes 'a knowable, unmysterious world ready to yield up its secrets to the patiently inquiring mind' can lead the way towards an abolition of idols and restoration of a quasi-prelapsarian condition (McVeagh, 1990: 9). In *Micrographia* (1665), the Baconian Robert Hooke emphasised this enterprise of redressing the fall through learning: '[since] mankind fell by tasting of the forbidden Tree of Knowledge, so we, their Posterity, may be in part restor'd by the same way, not only by beholding and contemplating, but by tasting too those fruits of Natural knowledge, that were never yet forbidden' (b2r). In his early work *Of Education* (1644), Milton had similarly claimed that 'the end of learning is to repair the ruins of our first parents' (*CPW* 11: 366–7). In his later epics, however, it seems to be through divine intervention only that fallen human beings can perceive the world without a 'film' before their eyes (*PL* 11.412, 415). Indeed, the imperfection of human knowledge,

Adam's as well as the reader's, is taken into account by the narrator, who routinely 'compare[s]/Great things with small' (2.923–4; 10.307) and by archangel Raphael, who translates heavenly truth into 'the dialect of men' (5.761). This Miltonic system of 'accommodation' transforms spiritual truth into worldly metaphors, as a necessary adjustment in a fallen world (see Swaim, 1984). The wilful mendacity of Milton's tempter figures, Comus and Satan, likewise uses both visual and rhetorical strategies. Even angels succumb to the trumperies of optical illusion and 'guileful' speech (*PL* 9.567), as in the case of Uriel. The mendacity of evil is condoned by God, as a consequence of Milton's insistence, not only in *Areopagitica*, that virtue can be proven only by trial: 'the knowledge and survey of vice is in this world so necessary to the constituting of human virtue, and the scanning of error to the confirmation of truth' (*CPW* 2: 515). The upright and virtuous have to learn how to recognise and fend off evil, a learning process that includes initial defeat, owing to the gullibility of those who have not yet learned to be suspicious. Indeed, we as readers first encounter Satan as he is compared to the 'sea-beast/Leviathan' (1. 200–1), whom a mariner by night mistakes for an island, anchoring his ship in the monster's 'scaly rind' (1. 206). This story was traditional in medieval bestiaries and Renaissance emblem books (see Fowler, *PL*, ad 1.200–8) as an allegory of Satan's powers of deception and human beings' defective powers of perception.

While for Martin Luther the eye was more dangerous than the ear (it is through the *concupiscentia oculorum* that the devil operates most successfully; 1885, 343: 2), in Milton visuality can also be beneficial, as in the paradoxical 'inner light' of faith that guides the blind poet (and Satan tempts Eve through dreams and whispering in her ear). His fascination with new optical technologies, as well as his knowledge about their shortcomings, are evident in his discussions of astronomy in *Paradise Lost*. The Galileo motif 'represent[s] both the powers of mortal vision and its fallibility' (Boesky, 1997: 23; see also Friedman, 2002). The link between Satan's 'fraudulent temptation' (9.531) and his shape-shifting (from cherub to cormorant, toad and serpent) associates him with Archimago from the *Faerie Queene* (1590–1596), Edmund Spenser's creator of false images who is able to change shape at will. Satan manages to deceive archangel Uriel by employing both visual and rhetorical deceit: 'cast[ing] to change his proper shape' (3.634), he accosts him in the form of a 'stripling cherub' (3.636), with tales of his desire to see God's new creation. Echoing seventeenth-century defences of Eve, an authorial comment here explains that Uriel, although the 'sharpest sighted spirit of all in heaven' (3.691), is deceived because of his own 'uprightness':

> So spake the false dissembler unperceived;
> For neither man nor angel can discern
> Hypocrisy, the only evil that walks
> Invisible, except to God alone,
> By his permissive will, through heaven and earth:
> And oft though wisdom wake, suspicion sleeps
> At wisdom's gate, and to simplicity
> Resigns her charge, while goodness thinks no ill
> Where no ill seems: which now for once beguiled

Uriel, though regent of the sun, and held
The sharpest sighted spirit of all in heaven;
Who to the fraudulent imposter foul
In his uprightness answer thus returned.

(PL 3.681–93)

Indeed, Uriel even condones what is unseemly in the cherub's eagerness to see the earth, explicitly declaring that the desire to 'know/The works of God, thereby to glorify/The great work-master, leads to no excess/that reaches blame, but rather merits praise/The more it seems excess' (3.694–8). His Baconian praise of experiment and investigation recalls the purpose of human education as spelled out in Milton's earlier *Of Education* (1644): 'regaining to know God aright … by orderly conning over the visible and inferior creature' (*CPW* 2: 366–9). Some doubts are hidden in Uriel's phrasing ('excess'), but his good-natured intent to believe the best of the adventurous angel predominates. It is only later that he discovers his mistake, undeceived by observing Satan's 'furious gestures in the mount [Niphates]' ('Argument' to Book 4). Here the learning process has set in: Uriel adjusts his initial wrong judgement by adding new evidence – in this case, too late.

Eve is another prominent case study of innocence and its lack of suspicion. For her as well, the learning process which undeceives her sets in too late. It is her desire to learn and experience the world, in itself a positive impulse for the Baconian Milton, which makes her a prey to Satan's mendacity: although corresponding to the exemplary 'warfaring Christian' of *Areopagitica*, 'that … sallies out and sees her adversary' (*CPW* 2: 514), she is here made to pay dearly for her experience. Patrick Brantlinger sees curiosity as 'Satan's chief bait' (1972: 355), and it is Eve's sense of wonder about the speaking serpent which implicates her so deeply in his sophisticated rhetoric that she falls prey to 'fraudulent temptation' (*PL* 9.531). In the shape of a toad, Satan first 'assay[s] by his devilish art to reach/The organs of her fancy', there to inspire 'phantasms and dreams' as well as 'inordinate desires' (4.803, 807). Even though Ithuriel discovers him quickly, Eve has been touched. She recounts to Adam her troubled dream in which an unknown male figure (Satan) anticipates the fall: 'with venturous arm/He plucked, he tasted' (5.64–5; compare her own later fall at 9.780–1). In her dream, Eve partakes of the fruit that is held 'even to [her] mouth' (5.83), and while her own fall is erased from the dream narrative ('that I, methought/Could not but taste. Forthwith up to the clouds/With him I flew …, 5.85–7), it is sight, touch and smell that together sway her decision. Here Eve, whose 'initial response to the serpent', according to Karen Edwards, 'is a scientific one, entirely worthy of a new philosopher' (1999: 21), is equated again with the limiting, traditional figure of the sensuous female. In the case of the 'weak' woman, persuasion is strongest when carnal urges are addressed. Adam, disconcerted by her dream, tries to convince himself that 'evil *into the mind* of god or man/May come and go, so unapproved, and leave/No spot or blame behind' (5.117–20, my italics). By contrast, the crucial temptation interview will later conclude with Satan's rhetorical flourishes winning 'into [*Eve's] heart* too easy entrance' (9.734, my italics). It is part of Milton's construction of gender difference that Eve's 'heart' and not her 'mind' is here most directly concerned.

The narrative of temptation culminates, as in the anticipatory dream (see 5.85), when her 'appetite' is roused:

> Fixed on the fruit she gazed, which to behold
> Might tempt alone, and in her ears the sound
> Yet rung of his persuasive words, impregned
> With reason, to her seeming, and with truth;
> Meanwhile the hour of noon drew on, and waked
> An eager appetite … .
>
> (9.735–40)

Edwards sees Eve in *Paradise Lost* as a (potential, and hence failed) experimenter and Baconian new philosopher. At the beginning of Eve's confrontation with the serpent, she argues, 'her attitude perfectly combines experimental skepticism and open-mindedness' (1999: 36), and if only she had kept up this questioning spirit rather than succumb to her feelings of wonder and desire, knowledge and scepticism could have remained pure instruments for the glorification of the creator: 'The point is that Eve ought to have been more, not less, of an empiricist; she ought to have pitted her experiential knowledge more polemically against Satan's' (33). In addition, *Paradise Lost* does not condone female demands for 'equality' but sees them as part of women's unruly nature. This bias colours the entire foundational narrative of the fall; and indeed, after her fall Eve for the first time introduces proto-feminist thoughts. When thinking about whether or not to share the fruit with Adam, she briefly contemplates keeping it to herself: 'So to add what wants/In female sex, the more to draw his love, /And render me more equal, and perhaps, /A thing not undesirable, sometime/Superior; for inferior who is free?' (9.821–5). The tension between equality in marriage and Eve's submission to her husband is seen by James Grantham Turner as 'an irresolvable doubleness at the heart of Milton's apprehension of wedded love – a contradiction that lies dormant in Genesis and the Pauline tradition' (1987: 286), and Mary Nyquist and Linda Gregerson have described Milton's Eve as essentially secondary to Adam and defined by her sensuality.[1] This kind of gender essentialism in part overwrites Eve's earlier positive spirit of inquiry which characterises her as a rational and educable human being – and which could have fortified her against mendacity. However, this reinscription of traditional clichés about female sensuousness does not seem to be part of Milton's depiction of the, of course explicitly virginal, Lady in the earlier *Comus*, as we will now see. Here he presents a female, rational and virtuous, whose ability to learn and thus withstand mendacity is one of her fundamental characteristics.

Comus: innocence learning suspicion

The Lady in *Comus*, walking in a wild wood 'with unacquainted feet' (l. 180), is equipped with education, the higher virtue of chastity and a quick ability to learn, all of which defend her against temptation to such an extent that after her initial mistake of misplaced trust, she quickly learns how to cut through the tempter's sophistries and reveal his warped logics. The masque was first performed on Michaelmas night 1634 to celebrate the Earl of Bridgewater's official inauguration as Lord Lieutenant of Wales – an office which also called upon him to 'keep … order and presid[e] over the Council, an important court of law that had been granted special jurisdiction over unlawful games, adultery and other sexual offences' (Marcus, 2001: 234). Comus embodies the period of festive misrule that is traditional for Michaelmas, and the masque's central virtue of chastity shows Bridgewater's children (a daughter and two sons), who acted in the masque, appropriately 'in victory over the local intemperance of Comus and his crew' (234). Chastity, in St Augustine's words, 'has its seat in the strength of the will, sustained by God's help, so that both body and spirit may be holy; and it is not a treasure which can be stolen without the mind's consent' (Augustine, 1984: 28; and see Lewalski, 1998: 312). The Lady celebrates the victory of mind over body in very similar terms in her address to Comus:

> … Fool do not boast,
> Thou canst not touch the freedom of my mind
> With all thy charms, although this corporal rind
> Thou hast immanacled, while heaven sees good.

> (ll. 661–4)

Daniel Colvin describes the Lady's plight as a representation of the audience's own spiritual predicament, as 'individuals placed in an arena to be tested for their own moral worthiness' (1978: 9). Even though she ends up immobilised in her chair, she has not accepted Comus's dangerous potion. Prefiguring Milton's Eve by several decades, the Lady also anticipates the 'second Eve', Mary, whose obedience to God's word is envisioned in *Paradise Lost* as the coming redemption (*PL* 10.183). While Eve's act is 'rash' – 'she plucked, she ate' (9.780, 781) – , Comus's aggressive attempt to produce a similarly spontaneous reaction in the Lady will fail: 'But this will cure all straight. /… /Be wise and taste. –' (ll. 811–13). The Lady seems to have all but reversed the fall through her education, her acquired (taught) virtues of commonsense and Protestant conceptions about chastity/virginity:[2] although fallen, she is paradoxically better equipped to withstand temptation than Eve in her pristine innocence. The 'dramatic fulfillment of [Comus's] defeat' (Colvin, 1978: 15) comes when the narrative is interrupted by the *dei* and *dea ex machina* (the brothers and the nymph Sabrina) at the crucial moment.

The Lady is educated and therefore less gullible, yet the dangers of the senses do remain a real threat. Eve is inveigled by a combination of sensual impressions and guileful rhetoric. In *Comus* the Lady, while immune to beguiling speeches, is initially deluded by 'false presentments' (l. 156), as Comus decides that in order to get his victim to listen he must first, with the help of his 'magic dust' (l. 165), 'cheat the eye with blear illusion' (l. 155). By disturbing the Lady's sense of sight, 'her natural means for distinguishing between good and evil, between appearance and reality', Comus thus also 'subvert[s] her understanding, a faculty which retained a vestigial capacity even after man's fall' (Colvin, 1978: 9). While Carol Scheidenhelm argues that there is a 'visual austerity' to the masque as 'Milton was primarily concerned with what went on within the character's mind' (1992: 59), it is significant that the Lady – like Eve – is initially captivated by visions. Indeed, Barbara Lewalski points out that Comus's visual trumperies and disguise stage 'the problem of deception and illusion in a fallen world where external form does not (in Neoplatonic fashion) reflect internal worth, and the fallacy of expecting the easy conquest or expulsion of evil usual in court masques' (1998: 307). As with Eve in her dream, the Lady is at first touched – the noise from Comus's crew produces 'a thousand fancies' in her mind, 'calling shapes, and beck'ning shadows dire' (ll. 205–7).[3] Presenting himself disguised as 'some harmless villager' offering to give the Lady shelter in his 'low/But loyal cottage' (ll. 180, 335–6), Comus manages to deceive her innocence. Here, as elsewhere in Milton, 'evil works by assuming the very form and reason of good', as Rosemond Tuve has argued (1962: 127). It is only after he has led her to what in fact is his *stately palace* (Stage Direction l. 658), filled with luxurious wastefulness and the strange beast hybrids of his entourage – 'a none-too-subtle allusion to the licentious Cavaliers' (Lewalski, 1998: 309; see Brown, 1985: 64–5) – that the Lady recognises her mistake, and him as a 'false traitor' (l. 689). Here the learning process sets in, which consists of the correcting of initial assumptions in the light of new evidence: 'although [he] does not realize it, by bringing the Lady to the palace, he has made seduction more difficult, if not impossible, because he has unwittingly helped her see evil for what it is' (Colvin, 1978: 13).

Comus's attempts at seduction continue through speech, and his hypocritical *carpe diem* plea for 'using' nature (and sexuality) resembles Satan's mendacious strategy which also exploits extant ambivalences and wonder in the first humans. The much-rehearsed debate between Comus and the Lady about the respective merits of conspicuous consumption and indulgence (Comus) versus frugality and 'spare temperance' (Lady) summarises a debate that is taken up by Eve and Adam in *Paradise Lost* (see 4.655–6; 8.26–8). Again, moral positions are not as clear-cut as they seem, owing to the close associations of Comus's arguments with the biblical parable of the talents, which similarly advocates the enjoyment of God's gifts for the glorification of their maker (see Marcus, 2001: 240). Comus only slightly modulates this idea, erasing God and appealing to the senses: 'Wherefore did Nature pour her bounties forth, / ... /But all to please, and sate the curious taste?' (ll. 709–13). While Scheidenhelm sees Comus as 'surprised and puzzled by the Lady's resistance to what seems to him a perfectly rational theory of nature's intent' (1992: 63), it is more convincing to see his rhetoric as deliberate mendacity. According to William Shullenberger, Comus's argument is founded on a conceit of *'trompe l'esprit'*: 'the Lady is invited to enjoy Nature's wealth at the same time that the invitation ... mak[es] her ... an object of enjoyment'. The same line of argument will be pursued by Satan in his seduction of Eve, and in both cases the 'specious logic tries to seal off objections or questions before they can be raised' (Shullenberger, 2008: 169). Comus's/Satan's voyeurism and eroticisation of the courted female also hope for the kind of subliminal response that the post-Restoration Milton would have associated with refined belles at the depraved Cavalier court. Yet, in contrast to Eve, the Lady fails to respond. Her reply is based on her learning process and reasoning power while also expressing the stance of virtuous goodness that is the staple of more conventional masques. Comus claims promptly that he 'fear[s]/Her words set off by some superior power' (ll. 799–800). Although still physically ensnared, the Lady is now undeceived.

The crucial moment of *anagnorisis* about the 'ease with which Comus has deceived her', cut from the performance text (probably so as not to compromise the performing young lady, see Marcus, 2001: 234), appeared in the published version of 1637:

> Hence with thy brewed enchantments, foul deceiver,
> Hast thou betrayed my credulous innocence
> With vizored falsehood, and base forgery,
> And wouldst thou seek again to trap me here
> With liquorish baits fit to ensnare a brute?

(ll. 696–700)

Here, again in contrast to Eve, the Lady has reached a point in her learning process which enables her to speak about her own former, innocent self in the past tense. Now undeceived, she will never again succumb to lying tempters. Still, Milton's masque is unsettling in its treatment of moral allegory, which departs significantly from the usual clear-cut oppositions offered in court masques or the traditional series of dances that form an 'allegory of the triumph of virtue over vice' (Scheidenhelm, 1992: 59). Leah Marcus has argued that 'the enchanter does not appear "up front" at the beginning of the masque, as would be expected of the typical courtly antimasque, where vice can be readily and safely identified'; she sees him as 'enfolded deep within a "drear wood", and within a series of lies and disguises that are impenetrable even to the virtuous except through sad experience' (Marcus, 2001: 239). However, while on the diegetic level the Lady is at first deceived by the pretence of righteousness, the audience is left in no doubt about Comus's evil nature from his initial monologue onwards where, in the tradition of the dramatic villain, he discloses his 'nature' and plans. Yet in contrast to traditional court masques, the Lady is an 'everywoman' rather than a combination of allegorical meanings;[4] she represents 'herself, Alice Egerton, and stands in for every virtuous woman who has ever been thrown into a situation for which nothing in her past could prepare her' (239). As the seduction attempt develops through its successive stages, the Lady is called upon continually to reconnect with her learning and education and also to devise new techniques for dealing with new experiences, in a manner similar to the Baconian 'steps' prescribed by Milton's Raphael for human investigation: 'In contemplation of created things/By steps we may ascend to God' (*PL* 5.511–12). This singular and less formalised masque which fails to define in advance what virtuous conduct would be in any given situation, requires of its agents 'constant individual vigilance and careful judgement of every human encounter' (Marcus, 2001: 239). Indeed, evil is not entirely vanquished: Comus remains at liberty in the woods, probably on the look-out for his next victim. But the Lady and her brothers have stood the test and can return home from the liminal space of temptation and initiation. Mendacity has been shown to be powerless against innocence fortified by reason and knowledge.

The 'Battle of the Sexes': knowledge against mendacity

By performing her education in Christian virtue which protects her against mendacity, the Lady is participating in a dialogue with Aemilia Lanyer (*Salve Deus Rex Iudaeorum*, 1611), Rachel Speght (*Mortalities Memorandum*, 1621) and other female contestants in the pamphlet war of the 'Battle of the Sexes'. These writers had put forward the argument that a sound (moral) education for females could help in part to reverse the fall, and to fortify the innocent against the onslaught of mendacity. Their arguments are again linked to the claims of Baconians that humankind can be redeemed through education. Daringly literalising the name of the Tree of Knowledge, Lanyer in 'Eve's Apology in Defense of Woman', the central part of *Salve Deus Rex Iudaeorum*, argues that knowledge originates with Eve and womankind: 'Yet Men will boast of Knowledge, which he tooke/From *Eves* faire hand, as from a learned Booke' (Lanyer, 1611: ll. 807–8.) Even more radically and paradoxically, her narrator allies herself with Eve 'by also petitioning the serpent to be her guide to wisdom' (Lewalski, 1993: 231; see ll. 797–808). Lanyer contradicts male suspicions of women's virtuous learning, which she constructs as an antidote to the sinful corruption of male knowledge 'by describing the evil men who killed Christ as "unlearned"' (McGrath, 2002: 335–6). Similarly, Speght in the 'Dreame' part of *Mortalities Memorandum* presents an 'Eruditions garden' where women may truly learn, and where learning is seen as a divinely instituted way to individual salvation. As part of an allegorical *psychomachia* narrative, Speght here presents a counter-myth to Eden: 'Experience' directs the poet persona to employ the aid of 'Knowledge'. This is, however, only the good sort of knowledge which 'by labour is attain'd', in contrast to the biblical narrative about Eve (Speght, 1621: 4). Like other women writers advocating female education – and like Bacon and Milton with their similar religious justifications for learning and education – Speght argues that 'evils are withstood' through learning: '*the minde without it is not counted good*' (Speght, 1625: 8, italics in original; reference to Proverbs 19:2). But she goes even further in contending that female acquisition of knowledge can be turned to good use for the benefit of all Christian believers – again, enabling them to identify and resist mendacity.

Marcus insists on the 'special status' of *Comus* in the canon of Milton's works because of the masque's 'attention to, and sympathy for, women' and Milton's insistence that exposure to temptation does not automatically compromise a woman's honour, but that she can be fully healed and restored (Marcus, 2001: 245). Viewed together with his Lady's 'credulous innocence' (l. 697) which initially renders her incapable of divining the evil behind Comus's disguise and rhetoric, a close connection becomes apparent to the discourse of the *querelle des femmes*: there, too, the continuously rehashed myth of the inherent sinfulness of womankind was rewritten to explain Eve as more innocent, more unknowing (and also, in what is a problematic movement of self-defeat, 'weaker') than Adam. Without the aid of experience, Eve's helplessness before evil paradoxically reveals her as more innocent: Lanyer similarly claims that 'the Serpents craft had her abusde' (l. 781). Milton's Eve, too, explicitly declares herself the 'weaker' part of the first couple (*PL* 9.382), yet it is in Lanyer that 'Eve's credulity is presented as an innate tendency to believe and trust, that is, a disposition to faith – and thus her simple credulity links her to the receptive, humble faith that the Virgin Mary shows in receiving the visitation from God' (Guibbory, 1998: 200). Milton's insistence on Eve's sensuality and 'appetite' in *Paradise Lost* is all but absent in this version of the fall, and Lanyer firmly shifts the blame from Eve to Adam: 'Her fault though great, yet hee was most too blame; /What Weaknesse offerd, Strength might have refusde' (ll. 778–9).[5]

Lewalski claims that 'Lanyer's biblical exegesis would have been outrageous (by contemporary standards)' (1993: 231–2). Yet her famous conclusion, the proto-feminist demand for gender equality, 'Then let us have our Libertie again' (l. 825), is founded on a notion of the prelapsarian inferiority that had made Eve an easy prey to Satan's mendacity:

> Our Mother *Eve*, who tasted of the Tree,
> Giving to *Adam* what shee held most deare,
> Was simply good, and had no powre to see,
> The after-comming harme did not appeare:
> The subtile Serpent that our Sex betraide,
> Before our fall so sure a plot had laide.
> That undiscerning Ignorance perceav'd
> No guile, or craft that was by him intended;
> For had she knowne, of what we were bereav'd,
> To his request she had not condiscended.
> But she (poore soule) by cunning was deceav'd,
> No hurt therein her harmeless Heart intended.

(ll. 763–74)

In this version, Eve (like Milton's Eve figure) lacks the completed education of the Baconian experimenter, the 'powre to see' and anticipate, from experience, the 'after-coming harme'. By contrast, the Lady in *Comus*, through her superior acculturation, rhetorical training and acquired qualities of virtue, is paradoxically superior to Milton's Eve, and reiterates some aspects of the latter-day Eves and their claims for education that we encounter in 'Battle of the Sexes' pamphleteering. The Lady is able to fend off evil – not at first sight, but at second sight. She bases her eventual rejection of Comus's advances on the moral and didactic tenet that 'that which is not good, is not delicious/To a well-governed and wise appetite' (ll. 703–4). This presupposes that the distinction between 'good' and 'not good' has by then become clear. By contrast, Eve's 'eager appetite' (9.740) in *Paradise Lost* was not 'well-governed' but prompted her to pluck the fruit, reconfirming the traditional, misogynist notion that 'women's eyes are the root of all evil. When Eve looked, she began to desire knowledge, and with this desire, death entered into the world' (Snook, 2005: 124, summarising the contemporary debate in tracts by Richard Brathwait and others).

In contradistinction to this, the various stages of the temptation in *Comus*, rather than successively tightening their hold on the victim, enable the Lady to acquire an increasingly clear judgement of the situation as well as the means of resistance. Shullenberger interprets the masque as a rite of initiation for the Lady/ the performing Alice Egerton, and comments on her activation of her biblical and classical knowledge in order to withstand temptation: 'What may have been schoolbook training for her in her girlhood takes on new meaning ... as imaginative and ethical resources for creative self-protection, self-fashioning, and self-transcendence' (2008: 25). We are here offered, he claims, 'the extraordinary typological revision of the narrative of the Fall, in which the postlapsarian woman cast as a second Eve refutes and rebuffs her tempter, holding fast until she can be delivered from the bondage that flesh is heir to' (77). We might add that Milton thus invests the Lady with more power than he conceded to his later Eve: the heroine of the masque can be compared to the educated women envisaged by *querelle des femmes* writers in that through learning, she symbolically overcomes the ruin of our first parents. To a greater extent than Milton's Eve, it is the Lady of the masque who turns out the true Baconian sceptic, albeit one who, as Comus himself has to acknowledge, combines her own intelligence with the support of a 'superior power' (l. 800). In the tradition of the dramatic villain, he is thus finally forced to declare that the trial between truth and falsehood is over.

Conclusion: innocence *and* knowledge

The temptation of innocence and/or virtue, and the existential instruction that comes through resistance, is a recurrent motif in Milton's oeuvre. Throughout, it is closely linked to Milton's tenet from *Areopagitica* that only 'uncloister'd virtue', virtue that has the chance to test itself against the world and possible evil, is true virtue – even the first human beings were 'sufficient to have stood, though free to fall' (*PL* 3.99), as God in *Paradise Lost* sums up the paradox of free will. For Milton, the moral call to humankind was 'to ordain wisely as in this world of evill, in the midd'st whereof God hath plac't us unavoidably' (*CPW* 2: 526). Deception in a fallen world results from an over-reliance on one's own senses and hermeneutic capabilities: Milton denies the possibility of any fixed 'settlement' on earth; on the contrary, he postulates a 'perpetuall progression' – 'he who thinks we are to pitch our tent here, and have attain'd the utmost prospect of reformation, ... that man by this very opinion declares, that he is yet farre short of Truth' (*CPW* 2: 549). The search for truth on earth consists in a continual, flexible movement from 'brotherly dissimilitudes' to 'neighboring differences', which remains alive throughout to the limitations of human perception (*CPW* 2: 555; 565). Milton terms this process, which has strong links to the Baconian method of investigation, 'knowledge in the making', claiming that it will continue until our 'Masters second coming' (*CPW* 2: 554; 549).

Unmasked and addressed by Christ in *Paradise Regained* as 'composed of lies/ From the beginning, and in lies wilt end' (*PR* 1.407–8), Milton's Satan and Comus have here been used as case studies for testing inquiries into early modern epistemologies, Baconian scepticism and proto-feminism. In Milton, mendacious rhetoric is usually exposed to the reader through the epic narrator's evaluating comments ('So spake ...') and epitheta assigned to the speaker ('fraudulent', 'guileful', 'wily', *PL* 9.531; 9.567; 9.625). To the masque audience, evil is revealed through the monological self-revelation of the dramatic villain – even though in both cases the diegetic victim might be ensnared. Thereby Milton's readers and audience are safeguarded from falling into the same traps as Uriel and Eve, or, briefly, the Lady (while they might, of course, as Stanley Fish has demonstrated in his now-classic *Surprised by Sin* [1967], be allowed to see the attractiveness of the promised rewards of sin, and understand why the 'righteous' had to err). Of course, in *Paradise Regained* Christ's answer to mendacity is and must be to repudiate the temptations of both 'eyes' and 'ear': 'Much ostentation vain ... /Before mine eyes thou hast set; and in my ear/Vented much policy, and projects deep/ ... /Plausible to the world, to me worth naught' (*PR* 3.87–93).

The situation is more complex in *Comus* and *Paradise Lost*: both texts, as we have seen, show innocence confronted by mendacity. But the Lady's astute analysis of Comus's mendacious rhetoric, while anticipating the moment of Eve's temptation in the later epic, far surpasses Eve's incomplete exertion of Baconian reason. Michael Lieb sees the masque as proposing 'a naive idealization of chastity's strength that the mature tragic poet of *Paradise Lost* would lament as insufficient to the deadly challenge of a fallen world' (1984: 110–11); and indeed, by the time we reach *Paradise Lost*, discourse about gender has shifted. On the one hand, we encounter here more essentialist differentiations that equate Adam with the more reasonable, Eve with the more sensual half of the first couple, and on the other hand the text seems to engage in negotiations with proto-feminist arguments that are far from welcoming of the female desire to be educated and 'equal' (compare Eve's rebellion after her fall, 'for inferior who is free?', *PL* 9.825). The ability to unmask mendacity here seems to be dependent on gender (and hence social) status.

Shannon Miller has argued that 'even though Eve's defense is overridden, and overwritten, in the course of the poem, the traces of that debate resonate through the language in the text' (2008: 47). Yet the fact remains that it is a postlapsarian Eve who starts speaking like Lanyer and Speght. For Milton, who did after all cling to a hierarchical idea of human community, such revolutionary utterances are an effect of the fall, and thus an extension of the initial deception. His Baconian insistence on observing and learning from *Of Education* extends to women only by implication. Glimpses of a Baconian educated female philosopher are offered with the example of the Lady, and with Eve's initial questioning of the serpent, but these visions are submerged in the more traditional image of Eve's 'eager appetite'. Satan's mendacious admiration of Eve as 'goddess among gods' (9.547) can be seen as a continuation of his own refusal to acknowledge hierarchies in heaven, and it produces, from the epic's perspective, both the fall and the ensuing 'Battle of the Sexes'. Comus's mendacity, by contrast, is inefficacious when he proposes to the Lady that 'she shall be my Queen' (l. 264). As a latter-day Eve, fortified by sound education and Protestant morality, the Lady translates virtue into chastity and obedience, thereby helping to 'redeem the fall'. While her final attainment of self-knowledge is thus not placed in a revolutionary context in social or political terms, the masque's emphasis on her learning and acquired virtue, perhaps surprisingly, coincides with proto-feminist justifications for female education. Mendacity, as the Milton of the masque and the women pamphleteers argue, is helpless before this paradoxical combination of prelapsarian and postlapsarian states: innocence *and* knowledge.

Disclosure statement

No potential conflict of interest was reported by the author.

Notes

1. See Nyquist (1987); compare Gregerson (1995: 196), who sees Eve, because of her 'secondariness' to Adam, as the 'normative' postlapsarian subject.
2. Notions of Milton's 'Puritanism', by contrast, have been shown to be inaccurate (see Martin, 2010).
3. Comus has been linked to the force of 'mimic fancy', identified by Robert Burton in *The Anatomy of Melancholy*, which Adam thinks inspired Eve's dangerous dream (*PL* 5.110), and to Spenser's 'false genius' (see Hieatt, 1964). See also Fowler, *PL* 5.102–9.
4. See Marcus (2001: 239) on references to Una from Spenser's *Faerie Queene* and to the Woman in the Wilderness from the *Book of Revelation*.
5. Compare Egerton (1686: n.p.): 'The Devil's Strength weak Woman might deceive, / But *Adam* tempted only was by *Eve*./*Eve* had the strongest Tempter, and least Charge;/Man's knowing most, doth his Sin make most large.'

References

St Augustine of Hippo (1984). *Concerning the City of God against the Pagans*. Trans. Henry Bettenson. Ed. John O'Meara. London: Penguin.

Bacon, Francis (1620). *Novum Organum*. Ed. and Trans. Basil Montague. Francis Bacon: The Works, 3 vols. Philadelphia, PA: Parry & MacMillan, 1854. Vol. 3. 343–71.

Beilin, Elaine V. (1987). *Redeeming Eve: Women Writers of the English Renaissance*. Princeton: Princeton UP.

Boesky, Amy (1997). 'Milton, Galileo, and Sunspots: Optics and Certainty in *Paradise Lost*.' *Milton Studies* 34: 23–43.

Brantlinger, Patrick (1972). 'To See New Worlds Curiosity in Paradise Lost.' *Modern Language Quarterly* 33: 355–69.

Brown, Cedric Clive (1985). *John Milton's Aristocratic Entertainments*. Cambridge: Cambridge UP.

Colvin, Daniel L. (1978). 'Milton's Comus and the Pattern of Human Temptation.' *Christianity and Literature* 27.3: 8–17.

Duran, Angelica (2005). The Age of Milton and the Scientific Revolution. Pittsburgh, PA: Duquesne UP.

Edwards, Karen L. (1999). *Milton and the Natural World: Science and Poetry in Paradise Lost*. Cambridge: Cambridge UP.

Egerton, Sarah Fyge (1686). 'The Female Advocate; or, an Answer to a Late Satyr against the Pride, Lust and Inconstancy of Woman.' *The Early Modern English-woman: A Facsimile Library of Essential Works*. General Eds Betty S. Travitsky and Anne Lake Prescott. Vol. Ed. Robert C. Evans. Aldershot: Ashgate, 2012.

Fish, Stanley E. (1967). *Surprised by Sin: The Reader in Paradise Lost*. London: Macmillan.

Friedman, Donald (2002). 'Galileo and the Art of Seeing.' *John Milton: Twentieth-Century Perspectives*. Ed. Martin Evans. New York: Taylor & Francis. 93–108.

Gregerson, Linda (1995). *The Reformation of the Subject: Spenser, Milton, and the English Protestant Epic*. Cambridge: Cambridge UP.

Guibbory, Achsah (1998). 'The Gospel according to Aemilia: Women and the Sacred.' *Aemilia Lanyer: Gender, Genre, and the Canon*. Ed. Marshall Grossman. Lexington, KY: U of Kentucky P. 191–211.

Hieatt, A. Kent (1964). 'Milton's *Comus* and Spenser's False Genius.' *University of Toronto Quarterly* 38.4: 313–8.

Hooke, Robert (1665). *Micrographia: Or Some Physiological Descriptions of Minute Bodies Made by Magnifying Glasses, with Observations and Inquiries Thereupon*. London: Martyn.

Lanyer, Aemilia (1611). 'Salve Deus Rex Judaeorum.' *The Poems of Aemilia Lanyer*. Ed. Susanne Woods. New York: Oxford UP, 1993. 3–127.

Lewalski, Barbara Kiefer (1993). *Writing Women in Jacobean England*. Cambridge, MA: Harvard UP.

Lewalski, Barbara Kiefer (1998). 'Milton's *Comus* and the Politics of Masquing.' *The Politics of the Stuart Court Masque*. Eds David Bevington and Peter Holbrook. Cambridge: Cambridge UP. 296–320.

Lieb, Michael (1984). *Milton and the Culture of Violence*. Ithaca: Cornell UP.

Luther, Martin (1885). *Werke: Kritische Ausgabe*. 120 Bde. Weimar: Preußisches Bildungsministerium/Heidelberger Akademie der Wissenschaften. Vol. 3. 1883–2009.

Marcus, Leah S. (2001). 'John Milton's *Comus*.' *A Companion to Milton*. Ed. Thomas N. Corns. Oxford: Blackwell. 232–45.

Martin, Catherine Gimelli (2007). 'Rewriting the Revolution: Milton, Bacon, and the Royal Society Rhetoricians.' *Science, Literature and Rhetoric in Early Modern England*. Eds Juliet Cummins and David Burchell. Aldershot: Ashgate. 97–123.

Martin, Catherine Gimelli (2010). *Milton among the Puritans: The Case for Historical Revisionism*. Aldershot: Ashgate.

McGrath, Lynette (2002). *Subjectivity and Women's Poetry in Early Modern England*. Aldershot: Ashgate.

McVeagh, John, ed. (1990). *All before Them: 1660–1780. English Literature and the Wider World, Vol. 1*. London: Ashfield Press.

Miller, Shannon (2008). *Engendering the Fall: John Milton and Seventeenth-Century Women Writers*. Philadelphia, PA: U of Pennsylvania P.

Milton, John (1634/37). 'A Masque Presented at Ludlow Castle.' *Milton: Complete Shorter Poems*. Ed. John Carey. 2nd ed. London: Longman, 1997. 173–234.

Milton, John (1667/1674). *Paradise Lost*. Ed. Alastair Fowler. 2nd ed. London: Longman, 1998. [PL].

Milton, John (1671). *Paradise Regained*. In Milton: Complete Shorter Poems. Ed. John Carey. 2nd ed. London: Longman, 1997. 417–512. [PR].

Milton, John (1953–1982). *The Yale Complete Prose Works of John Milton*. General Eds Don M. Wolfe et al. 8 vols. New Haven, CT: Yale UP. [CPW].

Nyquist, Mary (1987). 'The Genesis of Gendered Subjectivity in the Divorce Tracts and in *Paradise Lost*.' *Re-Membering Milton: Essays on the Texts and Traditions*. Eds Mary Nyquist and Margaret W Ferguson. New York: Methuen. 99–127.

Scheidenhelm, Carol (1992). '"Heav'n Hath Timely Tri'd [Her] Youth": Self-Knowledge through Language in Milton's *Comus*.' *Renaissance and Reformation* 28.3: 59–67.

Shullenberger, William (2008). *Lady in the Labyrinth: Milton's Comus as Initiation.* Madison, WI: Fairleigh Dickinson UP.

Snook, Edith (2005). *Women, Reading, and the Cultural Politics of Early Modern England.* Aldershot: Ashgate.

Speght, Rachel (1621). Mortalities Memorandum, with a Dreame Prefixed. London. Repr. in *The Early Modern Englishwoman: A Facsimile Library of Essential Works. Series I: Printed Writings, 1500–640.* Part 2, Vol. 10. Eds Susanne Woods, S. Betty Travitsky and Patrick Cullen. Aldershot: Ashgate, 2001.

Swaim, Kathleen M. (1984). 'The Mimesis of Accommodation in Book 3 of *Paradise Lost.*' *Philological Quarterly* 63: 461–75.

Travitsky, Betty S. and Anne Lake Prescott, General eds (2007–2008). *Texts from the Querelle. 3 vols. The Early Modern Englishwoman: A Facsimile Library of Essential Works.* Series III, Part 2, 1–3. Aldershot: Ashgate.

Turner, James Grantham (1987). *One Flesh: Paradisal Marriage and Sexual Relations in the Age of Milton.* Oxford: Clarendon.

Tuve, Rosemond (1962). 'Image, Form and Theme in *a Masque.*' *Images and Themes in Five Poems by Milton.* Cambridge, MA: Harvard UP.

Woodbridge, Linda (1984). *Women and the English Renaissance: Literature and the Nature of Womankind, 1540–1620.* Champaign, IL: U of Illinois P. 112–61.

Anne-Julia Zwierlein holds the Chair of English Literature and Culture at the University of Regensburg. She specialises in early modern and Victorian studies and has published widely on English literature and culture from the sixteenth century to the present. She is the author of *Majestick Milton: British Imperial Expansion and Transformations of Paradise Lost, 1667–1837* (LIT, 2001) and *Der physiologische Bildungsroman im 19. Jahrhundert* (Winter, 2009). Among her recent publications are the co-edited volumes *Interdisciplinary Perspectives on Aging in Nineteenth-Century Culture* (with Katharina Boehm and Anna Farkas, Routledge, 2014) and *Gender and Disease in Literary and Medical Cultures* (with Iris Heid, Winter, 2014), as well as a guest-edited special issue of *Zeitschrift für Anglistik and Amerikanistik* on Victorian oral cultures (2015). She is currently engaged in a project on Victorian oral and print mass cultures, which is funded by the German Research Foundation (DFG).

Brean Hammond and Gregory Currie

LYING, LANGUAGE AND INTENTION: REFLECTIONS ON SWIFT

This article, a literary and philosophical dialogue on lying in the eighteenth century and beyond, uses the writings of Jonathan Swift as a springboard for an interdisciplinary conversation on the truth conditions of human (and Houyhnhnm) communication. In the first two sections, Brean Hammond examines the cultural and political conditions that produced Swift's anxiety over a polity he considered to be riddled with untruth, leading to his imagining, in Gulliver's Travels, *a species incapable of lying. In the final section, Gregory Currie considers Swift's conception of creatures only able to tell truth — the Houyhnhnms — from a modern philosophical standpoint. Lying is deceptive wrongness and is as universally deplored as it is practised. The Houyhnhnms in Swift's* Gulliver's Travels, *who have no inclination to lie and find it hard even to understand mendacity in the abstract, are a literary rebuke to human shortcomings in this regard. What do they tell us about Swift's attitude to truth and falsity in the context of early eighteenth-century politics and imaginative writing? What role does intention play in the unfailing linguistic truthfulness of the Houyhnhnms? And what would a language be like in which one could not lie?*

BH: When it was suggested that I should contribute a piece focussed on the eighteenth century to a special number of *EJES* concerned with the topic of mendacity, my thoughts turned immediately to Jonathan Swift. Swift's success as a political writer for *The Examiner* depended on persuading a wide section of the reading public that partisan propaganda was verifiable truth. Only by achieving this would Swift cease to preach to the converted and start *making* converts: to the view that Marlborough and the Whigs *really were* wantonly expending human lives to prolong a war waged for their personal gain. Despite that success, Swift would continue to be haunted by the spectre of having his version of events dismissed as mere propaganda — as a self-interested, biased and partial account of history. Behind Swift's long aspiration to be Historiographer Royal was the desire to write an account of events so limpid, so clean, so free from any form of interference, so untouched by dirt and white noise, that it would have to be accepted by all readers as *true*. To disagree with Swift's version of events, therefore, would not simply be to hold a different opinion. To disagree with Swift, you would be a *liar*. Anyone who has read his *History of the Four Last Years of the Queen* knows just how far from that ideal his writing fell.

The intention behind the celebrated Book IV of *Gulliver's Travels* was to invent an order of being that *could not* lie, whose linguistic system was so calibrated that it could not be used for 'saying the thing that is not'. What kind of being would that language restriction then dictate? How viable is a linguistic system in which telling lies is impossible? What forms of communication does that rule in and out? During Swift's lifetime, philosophers were turning their attention towards the question of what makes propositions true. Lying, they would discover, is not merely a matter of getting things wrong. Nor is all culpable wrongness lying, since one can be culpably credulous or cavalier with the evidence without lying. Lying is deceptive wrongness and is as universally deplored as it is practised. Swift's Houyhnhnms, who have no inclination to lie and find it hard even to understand, are a literary rebuke to our own failings in this. What do they tell us about Swift's attitude to truth and falsity in the context of early eighteenth-century politics and imaginative writing? And what role does *intention* play in the unfailing linguistic truthfulness of the Houyhnhnms?

I found that I needed a modern philosophical perspective on these questions, so I turned to my colleague Gregory Currie. Greg is a philosopher whose special interest lies in problems that can be construed as philosophical arising in imaginative writing. He and I had previously discussed aesthetic issues in Shakespeare's period and writing. I had already found that my interest in the cultural conditions that create imaginative writing was valuably complemented and challenged by his interest in how that writing stands up to modern and contemporary forms of philosophical interrogation. The clarity of Greg's questions and the sharpness of his focus, deriving from a different methodology, had frequently trimmed the greater luxuriance of my own forms of historicising. How would his mind play over the questions raised by Jonathan Swift's obsessive search for truth?

With the permission and constructive support of the volume's general editors, we conceived this piece, unusually for the volume as a whole, in dialogue form, with me writing Section I of the article and Greg responding to those aspects of my argument that come within his sphere of interest, in Section II. We hope that the result leads on to further questions that prolong the dialogue in readers' minds.

I

My master heard me with great Appearances of Uneasiness in his Countenance; because *Doubting* or *not believing*, are so little known in this Country, that the Inhabitants cannot tell how to behave themselves under such Circumstances. And I remember in frequent Discourses with my Master concerning the Nature of Manhood, in other Parts of the World, having Occasion to talk of *Lying*, and *false Representation*, it was with much Difficulty that he comprehended what I meant; although he had otherwise a most acute Judgment. For he argued thus; That the Use of Speech was to make us understand one another, and to receive Information of Facts; now if any one *said the Thing which was not*, these Ends were defeated; because I cannot properly be said to understand him; and I am so far from receiving Information, that he leaves me worse than in Ignorance; for I am led to believe a Thing *Black* when it is *White*, and *Short* when it is *Long*. And these were all the Notions he had concerning that Faculty of *Lying*, so perfectly well understood, and so universally practised among human Creatures.

Thus opens chapter IV of Part IV of Swift's *Travels into Several Remote Nations of the World* (commonly known as *Gulliver's Travels*) in Faulkner's 1735 edition (Swift, 2012: 354). The words 'and so universally practised' had not appeared in earlier editions. Adding them, Swift stuck the needle deeper into his readers' *amour propre* by further emphasising the human facility for lying. Lying isn't just a conceptual achievement amongst humans: it is also what philosophers might describe as a 'dispositional' ability – a competence that can be actualised by humans at any time, and frequently is so.

The 1735 edition of *Gulliver's Travels* made the question of the narrative's truth-to-fact a much larger and more vexed one than had the 1726 Motte edition. Before encountering a single word of the story, the reader sees a pictorial representation of its supposed author/teller, 'Capt. Lemuel Gulliver', which in the depicted features, orientation of the head and costume details, bears an uncanny resemblance to George Vertue's engraving of the real-life Jonathan Swift, after the well-known Charles Jervas portrait. From the first, the reader is confused about who the 'real' author of this travel book is, and about whether it is a real travel book. Taken together, the obfuscations render problematic the distinction between fact and fiction, and that between truth and lies. That latter distinction is raised, and problematised, by the caption on the portrait of Gulliver, 'Splendide Mendax. Hor.', which, as Swift's latest editor David Womersley informs us, is taken from Horace's *Odes* III.xi.35 and means 'gloriously false' (Swift, 2012: 4).[1] If Gulliver is a fake, or the story he tells is a fabrication, it is, we are encouraged to believe, in some sense a virtuous, or 'glorious' deception.

The 1735 edition comes equipped with prefatory material from which 1726 readers did not benefit, and its accumulated effect is to further destabilise the reader's ability to distinguish between what is true and what is deliberately false in the text. Is this book factual or fictional? We start with an Advertisement which tells us about 'Mr. Sympson's *Letter to Captain Gulliver*' but actually, it is a letter from Captain Gulliver to Mr Sympson that the text contains. What is this – a slip, or a deliberate error? The Advertisement is very difficult to make out, but its overall effect is to set us wondering whether the text we are about to embark upon is actually the real text, as Swift intended it, or a text still containing errors and misprints carrying over from the 1726 Motte edition. The following 'Letter from Capt. Gulliver, to his Cousin Sympson' appears to reinforce the title page's claim that there is a real Lemuel Gulliver, who has a real cousin called Sympson (though the name is oddly spelt). Gulliver claims in this letter that William Dampier, a famous buccaneer and explorer who really *had* published a highly influential account of his travels called *A New Voyage Round the World* in 1697, is his cousin. And there follow a series of references that anticipate the story in a wholly mysterious way. We hear about 'my Master *Houyhnhnm*' and about *Yahoos* before we can have any idea what these exotic names can signify. Very uncomfortably, we come to discern that Gulliver somehow doesn't consider himself to be a member of the human race, because he speaks of it as though he were not included in it.

Capt. Gulliver's first major concern in the letter is that the first edition of the text is a mingle-mangle. At one point, we learn that the name *Brobdingnag* should actually have been *Brobdingrag*, unsettling because the name is itself difficult enough to pronounce without also having a misprint to reckon with. As Womersley astutely points out, Charles Ford's interleaved, annotated copy of the text, now in the Victoria & Albert Museum, does not list this as an error, so it is likely to be a 'bite', 'satirizing the very notion of literary correctness' (Swift, 2012: lxxxiii). Womersley fails to note that, in the King James Bible, the name of Nebuchadnezzar, King of Babylon, is in some books spelt thus, and in others spelt Nebuchadrezzar, so Swift may also be alluding to that relatively well-known crux concerning *n* and *r*. A reader who notices this is alerted, therefore, to the disconcerting fact that there are even textual cruces in the Scriptures themselves.

Gulliver's other major concern in his letter is that the wholesale reform of the human race that he expected his book to effect has not transpired. What is the reader to make of this absurd expectation that Gulliver's book would reform the human race? How can we regard such a naïve, utopian expectation as this, except perhaps as the raving of a lunatic? Having made their way through this preliminary material, original readers of *Gulliver's Travels* must have been very uncertain indeed about what they were about to read. 'The Publisher to the Reader' supplies us with more biographical information about Gulliver, and adds the detail that his name had become a byword for *veracity*: 'it became a Sort of Proverb among his Neighbours at *Redriff*, when any one affirmed a Thing, to say, it was as true as if Mr. *Gulliver* had spoke it'. So if you were beginning to suspect that the whole thing is a fiction, or even some kind of hoax, you have to confront a very aggressively expressed opinion that Lemuel Gulliver is the most truthful man who ever lived!

Clearly, then, when the reader reaches Part IV chapter IV, the question of lying is already imbricated in that of fact and fiction. In context, Gulliver has just been explaining to his 'master', a 'Sorrel Nag' – that is, a bright-chestnut-coloured riding pony (with a possible bawdy pun on 'nag' as a slang term for penis) – how he has arrived in Houyhnhnmland. What the Sorrel Nag finds difficult to credit is that Gulliver comes from a land where creatures who physically resemble the degenerate brutes that the Houyhnhnms call 'Yahoos' are in control, while creatures that resemble the Nag are enslaved for domestic labour. This novel psychological state perplexes the Nag, who is entirely unfamiliar with the sensations that accompany disbelief and has no experience of counterfactual propositions.[2] The paragraph puts pressure on readers from different, incompatible directions. Can a human reader conceive of language in a state of development so primitive (in the non-derogatory sense of originary) that untruth does not present itself as the indivisible verso of truth, the unmissable opportunity that framing any true proposition simultaneously offers? Such a language would surely be primitive in the derogatory sense: crude, unsophisticated – calling for a crowing response: 'And these were all the Notions he had concerning that Faculty of *Lying*, so perfectly well understood, and so universally practised among human Creatures.' So the paragraph ends in Gulliver inviting the human reader to glory in his ability to tell lies! Gulliver is enjoying his 'superiority', and only astute readers will construe this as ironic. Before naïve readers walk into this trap, they are invited to remain open to the possibility that there is something attractive about Houyhnhnm linguistics. Unevolved though such a language would be, Swift's contemporary reader might nevertheless find in it the same appeal as his contemporaries were increasingly locating in primitive poetry – its greater expressiveness and emotional intensity.[3] This, though, seems to be deliberately foreclosed, because, as Gulliver's 'Master', the Sorrel Nag, has told him in the passage quoted at the opening: 'the Use of Speech was to make us understand one another, and to receive Information of Facts'. This theory, seeming to anticipate early communication models of the twentieth century, such as that of Charles Osgood and Wilbur Schramm that concentrate on a receiver decoding the message of a transmitter, does not appear to allow for the complex set of speech acts, the distortions and noise, that enable the writing and understanding of fiction (Schramm, 1954).[4]

Womersley explores the background to this paragraph in an erudite note that commences by asserting that 'the Houyhnhnms' understanding of the purpose of language runs counter to the most advanced English thought on the subject published since the middle of the seventeenth century' (Swift, 2012: 356). 'Runs counter' seems inaccurate: more properly stated, Houyhnhnm linguistics are partial and selective, judged by the philosophical orthodoxy of the period. Hobbes and Locke both stressed that language distinguished men from beasts (as Womersley says, a relevant intellectual context for this part of *Gulliver's Travels*) and that it was capable of representing men's inner states, thus transcending solipsism. Houyhnhnms, one guesses, since they do not write, nor do they comprehend terms such as 'Opinion', would have little in the way of inner thought to communicate (Castle, 1980). The point being implied to the reader, rather, is that on Houyhnhnm linguistic theory, *Gulliver's Travels* itself could not be written. A century before Swift's birth, Sir Philip Sidney had distinguished poets from historians by arguing that 'for the poet, he nothing affirms, and therefore never lieth' (1973: 102). Sidney puts truth and lies into apposition where we might have expected truth and error, commencing a way of theorising about literature punningly summarised by Touchstone in *As You Like It*: 'the truest poetry is the most faining' (Shakespeare, 2006: 266).[5] Questions of genre are commingled here, as they are in *Gulliver's Travels*, with those of veracity.

Anxiety about truth-telling, overlapping with generic uncertainty, is provoked in Swift's writing career and in his lifetime by two epistemic challenges: that of writing 'true history' and that of writing fiction. I will argue that the two crises were for Swift and his era interrelated.

Swift lived through a period of war that, it is not exaggerated to say, defined England (and after 1707, Britain) as a modern nation: the War of the Spanish Succession. For the final four-year period of that conflict, he was extremely close to the most powerful men in the land – those who led the Tory administration of 1710–1714 and negotiated the Peace of Utrecht. For Swift, stating the true history of that war became a lifelong fixation. Amongst Swift's first inventions as editor of Robert Harley's Tory propaganda instrument *The Examiner*, was the idea that there was now an 'Art of *Political Lying*', the aetiology of which Swift supplied in *Examiner* 15 for 9 November 1710.[6] The social and political havoc that this art has wrought is described thus:

Considering that natural Disposition in many Men to *Lie*, and in Multitudes to *Believe*, I have been perplex'd what to do with that Maxim, so frequent in every Bodies Mouth, That *Truth will at last prevail*. Here, has this Island of ours, for the greatest part of twenty Years, lain under the Influence of such Counsels and Persons, whose Principle and Interest it was to corrupt our Manners, blind our Understandings, drain our Wealth, and in time destroy our Constitution both in Church and State; and we at last were brought to the very brink of Ruin; yet by the means of perpetual Misrepresentations, have never been able to distinguish between our Enemies and Friends. We have seen a great part of the Nation's Mony got into the Hands of those, who by their Birth, Education and Merit, could pretend no higher than to wear our Liveries.

(Swift, 1985: 24)

In *The Examiner*, Swift set out to persuade his readers that the war was being fought for the personal gain of a narrow Whig plutocracy led by the Duke of Marlborough. The creation of what recent historians designate the 'fiscal-military state' (a polity and its defences funded by the creation and servicing of national debt) resulted, Swift argued, in power and wealth migrating from landowners to financial investors (Brewer, 1989). Jumped-up footmen are now running the country. Whatever truth there was in the view repeatedly expressed by Swift and his mainly Tory contemporaries, that landowners were losing their power base to the money men, it is observable even from the brief extract supplied above that Swift's proto-Burkean conservatism postulates a binary approach: there are 'Enemies and Friends', there is 'Truth' and there are 'Misrepresentations'.

Two years later, in a satirical treatise called *Proposals for printing a very curious discourse, in two volumes in quarto, intitled, Pseudologia Politike; or, a treatise of the art of political lying* (1712), Swift developed the idea that there was a species of lying appropriately called 'political'.[7] This witty prospectus outlines the contents of an 11-chapter volume that first provides a comically mechanistic account of how the human body produces political lies, and goes on to prove them entirely lawful. Common people, the proposer reasons, are not entitled to be told the truth about politics: 'the People may as well all pretend to be Lords of Mannors and possess great Estates, as to have Truth told them in Matters of Government' (9). Nevertheless, the administration does not have a monopoly on political lies, and the people should be entitled to tell some for their own purposes. Developing the technique of the earlier *Examiner* essay, *The Art of Political Lying* divides lies into different species having different causes and utilities. It goes on to provide practical advice on how to tailor lies appropriately and how to ensure that they are believable. The proposer advocates lies that remain as faithful as possible to some conception of truth. There is advice on the spreading of political bugbears; and the accommodating suggestion that the Whigs could restore their credibility as political liars if they were to have a three-month amnesty on the telling of lies. The Swiftian character of the satire can be discerned in a passage such as the following, with its materialistic idea for the 'proving' of lies, and the gratuitous swipe at one of Swift's favourite stalking-horses, the Catholic doctrine of the Eucharist:

> Here the Author makes a Digression in Praise of the *Whig-Party,* for the right Understanding and Use of *Proof-Lyes.* A *Proof-Lye* is like a Proof-Charge for a Piece of Ordnance, to try a Standard-Credulity. Of such a nature he takes Transubstantiation to be in the Church of *Rome,* a Proof-Article, which if any one swallows, they are sure he will digest every thing else. (19)[8]

For the rest of his life, Swift, who coveted the position of Historiographer Royal, remained determined to tell the true history of those four years and despite discouragement from Lord Bolingbroke, a key witness to the period's events, he continued to write the *History of the Four Last Years of the Queen,* unpublished in his own lifetime and appearing in print first in 1758. This, unfortunately, is history as written by a Houyhnhnm – not in the sense that it is an expression of perfect rationality, but in the sense that Swift simply cannot see that there can be any room for opinion in an account of his nation's past. Swift believed that there was truth, and that he possessed it. He could not conceive that to those readers who did not approach the events of the period from his set of assumptions, he was *saying the thing that is not* when he attacked Marlborough, Wharton and their conduct of the war while venerating Robert Harley to the point of hagiography. He was close to power at a point when the structure of politics denied legitimacy to opposition. As late as 1715, Harley was arraigned and sent to the Tower when his administration fell: falling from power was its own punishment and *ipso facto* evidence of corruption in office. To oppose the government of the day was to be part of a narrow 'faction', not operating in the interests of the nation (Rogers, 1970; Jones, 2013). It is this understanding of political life that imposes such a binarism upon the conceptual apparatus with which politics was – and sometimes still is – thought.

Albeit punningly, the term 'faction' can provide a bridge between the historical and the literary challenges facing Swift in his time. If, as suggested above, the separation between truth and lies in contemporary historiography resulted from a conceptual matrix creating all opposition as 'faction', fiction too was, at the point of development reached in Swift's time, in a condition of 'faction'. Aspiring writers of prose fiction could not, with the insouciance that Sidney had displayed (as quoted above), deny making affirmations about the extra-fictional world and therefore they remained nervous about being accused of telling lies. Lies could, after all, have consequences in the real, extra-fictional world, in the form of prosecution for seditious libel. Many accounts of the novel's emergence and development in England, following that of Ian Watt, have been based on a distinction between the novel proper, characterised by its realism, and romance forms based ultimately on the classical epics – idealised in setting and character, aristocratic in focus and episodic in structure. Some years ago, Lennard Davis proposed that prose fiction destined to evolve into the novel derived from history and journalism, was middle-class, was concerned with present-day actuality and usually adopted the first person or epistolary form (Davis, 1983). Characteristic of this realist fiction is its claim to documentary status: it is more 'faction' than fiction. Typical in this respect is the uneasy Preface to Defoe's *Robinson Crusoe*, where a story that the title page claims is '*Written by Himself*' now turns out to have an editor:

> The Editor believes the thing to be a just History of Fact; neither is there any Appearance of Fiction in it: And however thinks ... that the Improvement of it, as well to the Diversion, as to the Instruction of the Reader, will be the same.

> (Defoe, 2010: 45)

So *Robinson Crusoe* purports to be an edited text rather than a whole-cloth fabrication, though the editor is eager to claim the classically respectable Horatian virtues of the *utile et dulce*, instruction and diversion (though not necessarily in that order), for his publication. Three years later, in *Moll Flanders* (1722), Defoe distinguishes what he is writing from both 'Novels' and 'Romances', calling his work a 'private History' and representing the text as a tidied-up version of the protagonist's own story, the protagonist being a real person (Defoe, 2004: 3). Well-known accounts of the story of the Scottish sailor Alexander Selkirk's isolation on Juan Fernandez, available in print shortly before *Robinson Crusoe* was published, further occluded the boundary between fiction – treating characters acting against a realistic background who never did so act and never existed – and documentary fact (Novak, 2001: 538–9).[9] Defoe appears to have thought fiction respectable only if it had a factual basis – if it did not float off into a Sidneian realm of non-referentiality. The duty of imaginative writing to instruct its reader could only be fulfilled if it was insulated from being a lie.

I have argued elsewhere the extent to which *Gulliver's Travels* is in parodic dialogue with *Robinson Crusoe*. One of Swift's many Defovian targets is the slippery tactic of positioning his fictional writing between fact and fiction, between truth and lies. If Defoe's fictions are, to invoke the title of Davis's (1983) book, 'factual fictions', then Swift's will be 'gloriously false' – which may mean that they will challenge the known laws of physics and assert physiological impossibilities such as the existence of Houyhnhnms. If, in his prefatory material, Defoe indirectly claims the respectable Horatian virtues for his text, Swift will take his motto, '*Vulgus abhorret ab his*', from Lucretius's materialist and atheist *De rerum natura* IV.19–20. Rather than being educated and instructed by the *Travels*, 'the people' will 'shrink away from it'. Returning to the passage with which we began this dialogue, another of the affronts it gives to the reader is the facility with which Gulliver begins to call the Houyhnhnm Sorrel Nag 'master': 'my Master heard me...'. This surely refers directly to the following passage in *Robinson Crusoe*:

> first, I made him know his Name should be *Friday*, which was the Day I sav'd his Life; I call'd him so for the Memory of the Time; I likewise taught him to say *Master*, and then let him know, that was to be my Name.

> (Defoe, 2010: 220)

In Swift, this is an aspect of a developing critique of Defoe's imperialist and colonialist assumptions. The progressive emancipation from 'faction' in *Gulliver's Travels*, its glorying in a fictionality that, simultaneously, it challenges the reader to disbelieve, its poking fun at realistic conventions that define the very nature of Defoe's achievement, is its hallmark as an original work. *Gulliver's Travels* is deliberately positioned between fact and fiction, between truth and pretence, and truth and lies, intentionally mystifying the grounds upon which such distinctions are made.

The castaway upon whom *Robinson Crusoe* is based was the Scots mariner Alexander Selkirk, and that Moll Flanders's story owes much to the biography of the confidence trickster Mary Carleton (Kietzman, 2004). Having their origins in true stories, they are in this additional sense 'factions'. Swift was more of a 'factionist' than his mockery of Defoe might suggest. When Swift tried his own hand at writing a historical novel, his neglected *The Memoirs of Capt. John Creichton* (1731), the story emerges as somewhere between a piece of ghost-writing and a wholesale fabrication (Hammond and Seager, 2009). John Creichton, the anti-Covenanter and loyal Jacobite, came into Swift's life when he resided at Market Hill as a guest of the Achesons in 1728–1729, and Swift could not resist writing up his tale of derring-do. *Gulliver's Travels* might owe its inspiration to a similar chance meeting with a larger-than-life real person. The protagonist's name, Lemuel Gulliver, appears to have been a very late addition to the text, gleaned by Swift on his 1727 visit to England when he stayed at an inn kept by one Samuel Gulliver. A title now considered iconic may have been conferred through mere happenstance. Adding to this impression of contingency, the true life individual upon whom Gulliver could have been modelled was possibly one Richard Coleire, whom Swift befriended in 1708 and who, as Swift's most recent biographer Leo Damrosch tells the story, 'was a young clergyman who was forced by bad financial management to leave his family and go to sea, was deserted on the shores of a strange land, and then had to make his way back to England' (Damrosch, 2013: 176; Treadwell, 1983). *Gulliver* too may be, at least in part, a 'faction'.

II

The role of intention

Swift's 1735 edition insists not merely on the possibility of lying among humans, but on its being a near-universal of conduct. We don't need to teach children to lie, though we do need to teach them the difference between lying in a good cause (otherwise known as tact) and lying for personal gain, and our tendency to mislead goes way beyond what we would strictly call lying: selective truth-telling, exaggeration, faked smiles etc. The Houyhnhnms on the other hand don't merely refrain from lying – it does not occur to them to lie. This characteristic serves evident rhetorical purposes for Swift, who wants a polar-opposite to human failing. But how are we to understand the Houyhnhnm incomprehension of lying? Gulliver's master seems to comprehend, if reluctantly, that humans do lie; what astonishes him is that (to put it in somewhat modern terms) a practice of lying can become stable in a community. For, to continue the extract quoted above, he says, 'the Use of Speech was to make us understand one another, and to receive Information of Facts; now if any one *said the Thing which was not*, these Ends were defeated; because I cannot properly be said to understand him; and I am so far from receiving Information, that he leaves me worse than in Ignorance' (Swift, 2012: 354). If it is common knowledge in a community of language users that people can and do lie, that surely undermines people's faith in the capacity of language to fulfil its function, much as the practice of using money is undermined by disbelief in its universal acceptability – so the thought goes. And elsewhere Swift adds fuel to this argument by insisting that, in certain quarters at least, lying is not merely a stable practice but the prevailing norm. Of lawyers he says (*GT* IV.v), 'there was a Society of Men among us, bred up from their Youth in the Art of proving by Words multiplied for the Purpose, that *White* is *Black,* and *Black* is *White,* according as they are paid. To this Society all the rest of the People are Slaves.' Why don't such things simply destroy language? One might quarrel with the Master's assertion that the purpose of language is to convey and receive '"information of facts"'. At best this looks like one purpose, another being the manipulation of other people.

Plausibly, language evolved to help us manage our social affairs; as Robin Dunbar (1996) argues, grooming did that for our distant ancestors but as social groups got larger, the time necessary to spend on grooming increased unmanageably and language emerged as another solution; by talking to people you could win them over, and winning people over is not always best achieved by telling the truth (Dunbar, 1996). But this is not fully an answer to Gulliver's Master for the problem remains – how would manipulation of others through language be possible, if language was known to be so unreliable a medium? The proper answer is that there is a delicate balance here, and that language users, by and large, maintain that balance. Lies may succeed in enhancing your reputation – but once discovered they destroy it. That means that lies will be resorted to, by and large, only when they confer great advantage or incur little risk. Also, human emotional ties dampen our tendency to lie by encouraging long-term commitments between people. So lying, while more common than we might like (and more common than Swift definitely does like), is not so common that the risks of being misinformed by language outweigh its usefulness. And if, as Swift supposes, there are situations where lying is the norm, they are kept within carefully circumscribed institutions like law courts, where complex rules of evidence prevail.

Gulliver's Master might be satisfied with this answer without being in the least tempted to engage in lying himself. Is lying a possibility for Houyhnhnms? Here I take an approach slightly different from Brean Hammond's: in my view the difference between Houyhnhnms and us is not a difference of language, but a difference of intention. Of course their language is different from ours, but not in ways that makes lying impossible in theirs. Gulliver spoke their language, and could have used it to mislead had he not, as he said, lost his own appetite for deception by being among them. And their language seems to be about as complex as ours, since Gulliver translates between the two.

What would a language that one could not lie in be like? Brean Hammond asks, 'Can a human reader conceive of language in a state of development so primitive (in the non-derogatory sense of originary) that untruth does not present itself as the indivisible verso of truth, the unmissable opportunity that framing any true proposition simultaneously offers?' The only examples I can think of are those signalling systems we find in certain animal species, where the ability to send the signal depends on having the very quality you are signalling; thus the peacock's elaborate tail reliably signals health and general fitness as a mate to peahens, because an unhealthy peacock simply can't sustain the cost in energy of an elaborate tail (see also the essay by Anna Swärdh in this issue). And such systems are surely *too* simple to count as proper languages (we can call all signalling systems languages if we like, but we are still going to need some way to distinguish the simple signals of peacocks from the complex, recursively generated messages of Houyhnhnms and humans). There cannot be a rule of language that prevents speaking grammatically but with deliberate untruth, just as there cannot be a gun which makes it impossible to shoot innocent bystanders. It is not, then, language per se which is the key to lying but intention, and anyway lying, or something next door to it, is possible without language; when reversing your car, you may depend on my holding my hands apart to indicate the space behind you, and it requires only malice for me to misrepresent the distance and wreck your car.[10] Lying comes in with communication, and communication is prior to language.

So the difference between Houyhnhnms and humans is not the structure of language but the structure of intention: we have intentions which they do not, and perhaps cannot, have. And intention is the key to something else in this debate: the fictionality or otherwise of Swift's story. Brean claims that various deliberate oddities in the presentation of Swift's text 'render problematic the distinction between fact and fiction, and that between truth and lies'. I agree, but I suggest we keep very salient that the fact/fiction boundary is not that between truth and lies. Brean does not, I think, want to conflate them, but for me the distinction is absolutely crucial and psychologically real for Swift's intended audience. I claim we all know, and always have known, the distinction between lies and fiction, and the reason goes back to the ubiquity of lying in our historical and pre-historic past referred to above. Here's the reason.

If language evolved as a tool for manipulating others, it surely created an intra-species arms race between deceivers and those who would like to avoid being deceived. That is, an arms race between everybody and everybody, since it's in everybody's interest to be a successful deceiver and to avoid succumbing to deception. That's why we are so highly attuned to the possibility that we are being deceived by another person, looking for clues in demeanour and expression, obsessively recalling previous lies, and attending closely to the testimony of others on this person's reliability. (The Houyhnhnms don't have those characteristics, but then their language – somehow – did not come about for purposes of manipulation.) But to be good judges of people's reliability we have also to make a distinction between utterances which are deceptively false and those which are false but non-deceptive. We do not, for example, want to write off as deceivers all those people who use conditionals with false antecedents, as in 'If Albert comes to the party there will be trouble', a statement which can be true and informative even if Albert does not come to the party, or who give indirect reports of thought and speech, as in 'I thought Albert went to the party'. We need, that is, a distinction between asserted and unasserted utterances, as the embedded 'Albert went to the party' is unasserted in the last example. So even before we bring fiction into the picture, competent users of an articulated language who want to benefit from embedding but to avoid being misled need a distinction between deceptive and undeceptive falsehood. Now my claim is that people will by dint of nature have at least most of what we regard as the intuitive distinction between fiction and nonfiction. For a fictional narrative is typically a sustained piece of false, undeceptive discourse. Of course there is more to learn about fiction than that, and to tell whether any given stretch of discourse is or is not fiction, one may need contextual clues as to the utterer's intentions. These may, in some cases, not be available, leaving us uncertain as to whether what we have is fiction or not. Perhaps that is why Robinson Crusoe is said to have confused readers and ultimately to have expanded readers' and writers' assumptions about what is legitimately the content of fiction. But it helps to recognise that the twists and turns in the history of fiction and its genres are constrained by the natural topography of the evolved human mind.

Disclosure statement

No potential conflict of interest was reported by the authors.

Notes

1. Womersley (in Swift, 2012: 4) alerts us to the fact that in the poem *The Life and Genuine Character of Dr Swift*, Swift twice attributes to a detractor the view that the 'travels' were lies.
2. Some 20 years later, David Hume would argue that the difference between the fictional and the factual resides entirely in the more 'vivid, lively, forcible, firm, steady conception of an object than what the imagination alone is ever able to attain', in other words in the feeling of belief engendered by what is factual. See Hume (1962: 66).
3. Two landmarks here are John Dennis's *The Advancement and Reformation of Modern Poetry* (1701), sponsoring ancient poetry for its passion and enthusiasm and laying the groundwork for Dennis's later work on Hebrew poetry; and Joseph Addison's *Spectator* papers devoted to a recuperation of the ballad, No. 70 for 21 May 1711 and 74 for 25 May 1711.
4. For non-code-based approaches influential in philosophy and linguistics see Grice (1986) and Sperber and Wilson (1995).
5. Shakespeare's *As You Like It* is a play structured on the relationship between poetry and lies, and in constant dialogue with Sidney's *Apology*. See Dusinberre's note to 3.3.15–16 in Shakespeare (2006: 266).
6. David Womersley is incorrect in stating that this is Number 14 (Swift, 2012: 355). Misnumbering of *The Examiner* occurs because in the first collected edition by the printer John Barber, number 13 was omitted.
7. This is commonly attributed to Arbuthnot, but it was printed in 1727 as part of the Pope-Swift *Miscellanies* and subsequently appeared in editions of Swift's complete works. On stylistic grounds, there are certainly reasons for attributing it to Swift. Its satiric structure is very close to that of Swift's earlier satires, as for

example *The Mechanical Operation of the Spirit* (1704) and *An Argument against... Abolishing Christianity* (1708).

8.   Compare *A Tale of a Tub*, Section 4, where the Catholic Peter is said to have 'an abominable Faculty of telling huge palpable *Lies* upon all Occasions; and swearing, not only to the Truth, but cursing the whole Company to Hell, if they pretended to make the least Scruple of believing Him' (Swift, 2010: 177).

9.   The story of the confidence trickster Mary Carleton was widely thought to be the basis for Defoe's characterisation of Moll Flanders.

10.   Why isn't such a signal linguistic? After all, there is sign language. But I am not invoking conventionalised hand signals here like the old-fashioned ones for turning left, but 'spur of the moment' signals as, in this case, I indicate the distance from the car behind (the example is due to Chomsky). That signal can be used and understood as a 'one off' even if never used again. It does not belong to any system of signs and is in no sense conventionalised.

References

Brewer, John (1989). *The Sinews of Power: War, Money and the English State, 1688–1783.* London: Unwin Hyman.

Castle, Terry (1980). 'Why the Houyhnhnms Don't Write: Swift, Satire and Fear of the Text.' *Essays in Literature* 7: 31–44.

Damrosch, Leo (2013). *Jonathan Swift: His Life and His World.* New Haven and London: Yale UP.

Davis, Lennard J. (1983). *Factual Fictions: The Origins of the English Novel.* New York: Columbia UP.

Defoe, Daniel (2004). *The Fortunes and Misfortunes of the Famous Moll Flanders, & C* (1722). Ed. Albert J. Rivero. New York and London: Norton.

Defoe, Daniel (2010). *The Life and Strange Surprizing Adventures of Robinson Crusoe* (1719). Ed. Evan R. Davis. Peterborough, Ontario: Broadview Press.

Dunbar, Robin (1996). *Grooming, Gossip, and the Evolution of Language.* Cambridge, MA: Harvard UP.

Grice, Paul (1986). *Studies in the Way of Words.* Cambridge, MA: Harvard UP.

Hammond, Brean S. and Seager, Nicholas (2009). 'Jonathan Swift's Historical Novel, the Memoirs of Capt. John Creichton (1731).' *Swift Studies* 24: 73–87.

Hume, David (1962). *An Inquiry concerning Human Understanding* (1748). Ed. Antony Flew. London and New York: Collier-Macmillan.

Jones, Tom (2013). 'Pope and the Ends of History: Faction, Atterbury, and Clarendon's *History of the Rebellion*.' *Studies in Philology* 110.4: 880–902.

Kietzman, Mary-Jo (2004). *The Self-Fashioning of an Early Modern Englishwoman: Mary Carleton's Lives.* Aldershot: Ashgate.

Novak, Maximillian (2001). *Daniel Defoe: Master of Fictions.* Oxford: Oxford UP.

Rogers, Pat (1970). 'Swift and Bolingbroke on Faction.' *Journal of British Studies* 9.2: 71–101.

Schramm, Wilbur (1954). How Communication Works. *The Process and Effects of Communication.* Urbana: U of Illinois P. 3–26.

Shakespeare, William (2006). *As You like It.* Ed. Juliet Dusinberre. *The Arden Shakespeare.* 3rd ed. London: Thomson.

Sidney, Sir Philip (1973). 'A Defence of Poetry.' *Miscellaneous Prose of Sir Philip Sidney.* Eds Katherine Duncan-Jones and Jan van Dorsten. Oxford: Clarendon Press. 73–121.

Sperber, Dan and Wilson, Deirdre (1995). *Relevance.* 2nd ed. Oxford: Oxford UP.

Swift, Jonathan (1985). *Swift Vs Mainwaring: The Examiner and the Medley.* Ed. Frank H Ellis. Oxford: Clarendon Press.

Swift, Jonathan (2010). *A Tale of a Tub and Other Works. The Cambridge Edition of the Works of Jonathan Swift* (2008-). Vol. 1. Ed. Marcus Walsh. Cambridge: Cambridge UP.

Swift, Jonathan (2012). *Gulliver's Travels. The Cambridge Edition of the Works of Jonathan Swift* (2008-). Vol. 16. Ed. David Womersley. Cambridge: CUP.

Treadwell, Michael (1983). 'Swift, Richard Coleire, and the Origins of *Gulliver's Travels.' Review of English Studies* 34: 304–11.

Brean Hammond is Emeritus Professor of English Literature at the University of Nottingham. He is the author of numerous books and articles on literature from 1590–1820, his main interests being in Shakespeare and the long eighteenth century. His most recent publications include *Jonathan Swift* (Irish Academic Press, 2010) and *Double Falsehood* (The Arden Shakespeare, 2010).

Greg Currie is Professor of Philosophy and Departmental Chair at the University of York. He works mostly on the arts and cognition. He recently co-edited two collections of essays on that topic: *Aesthetics and the Sciences of Mind* (Oxford University Press, 2014) and *Philosophical Aesthetics and the Sciences of Art* (Cambridge University Press, 2014). He is completing a book on literature and knowledge, to be published by Oxford University Press.

Index